BELSIZE 2000

A living suburb

BELSIZE
2000

A living suburb

Belsize Conservation Area Advisory Committee

Our special gratitude is due to the contributors to this book, both those who have kindly permitted us to re-use their contributions to the first edition, and those who have written articles for the present edition. Particular thanks are due to the members of the Belsize Conservation Area Advisory Committee.

We also acknowledge the kindness of the London Metropolitan Archive (and former GLC Architectural Department archive) for the use of photographs from their collection.

Published by the Belsize Conservation Area Advisory Committee,
12 Lawn Road, London NW3 2XS

Edited by Adrian Shire
Designed by Simon Loxley
Printed by Summit Print
ISBN 0-9539421-0-4

Belsize: a living suburb
The 1986 book
Editor Leonie Cohn, designer Rosalind Simon, cover by Jake Brown

The 1986 Exhibition Working Party
Gene Adams, Pamela Banchero, Jake Brown, Paul and Leonie Findlay, Mary Shenai

Belsize 2000: a living suburb
Millennium Project: Book & Exhibition Working Party:
Gene Adams, Margaret Finch, Mary Shenai and members of the committee: S A Cheifetz
(coopted treasurer), Gian Banchero, Patricia Brock, Nicole Charlet, Derek Kelley, Leonie Findlay,
Max Nasatyr, Kathryn Stubbs; other helpers: Margaret Wolfson, Michael White, Julie Anne Sadie,
Malcolm Holmes and Aidan Flood.

Picture captions
Cover: 108 Haverstock Hill, one of the houses saved by the Belpark initiative (JAKE BROWN)
Half-title page: 2 Fellows Road (GLC ARCHITECTURAL DEPARTMENT)
Title page: Street scene in Belsize Park, by Robert Bevan:
the junction of Belsize Park and Buckland Crescent (THE MUSEUM OF LONDON)

CONTENTS

* Articles marked thus are reprinted (some of them in a revised form) from the first, 1986 edition of this book.

The west window in St Peter's,
Belsize Square, depicting the
Ascension Memorial to
Edward Storey Middleton, who died
February 12th 1873 aged 31 (detail).

PHOTOGRAPH BY JAKE BROWN

Major sponsors of the exhibition and book Belsize 2000: A Living Suburb

Millennium Festival Awards for All
Belsize Residents Association
St Stephen's Trust
Photocraft (Hampstead)
London Borough of Camden

AWARDS FOR ALL

BELSIZE CAAC MILLENNIUM PROJECT

LOCAL BUSINESS AND PROFESSIONAL SUPPORTERS

Architects & artists
Michael Brod Associates
Flannery Architects
Ken Pyne
Hampstead Artists Council

Chemists & related businesses
Village Pharmacy
Alfred Aichin & Co.

Galleries & furnishers
Frame Factory
    (Haverstock Hill)
La Maison Creatif

Grocery stores & wine merchants
Crispins
Europa Foods

Hotels
Forte Post House Hotel
Marriott Hotel
Haverstock Arms

Medical & veterinary
The Veterinary Practice Group

Property & related
Hadleigh
Parkheath Estates Ltd

Undertakers
Leverton & Sons Ltd

Educational institutions
Lyndhurst House School
St Christopher's School

Local Association
Heath & Hampstead Society

INDIVIDUAL LOCAL SUPPORTERS

Gene Adams
Roy Allen
Patricia Angadi
Amit Batra
V Becker
Corinne Bellow
M Boltz
Lt-Col. Boyle and
    Mrs C L Boyle
Mrs V Bradsbaw
Caroline Brooks
John Burkett
S A Cheifetz
Raymond Chinnock
George Cleassen
Donna and David Cook
Sue Cook
Brian Doctor

Jackie Ennals
Mr & Mrs Ettinger
Richard and
    Margaret Finch
Leonie Findlay
Chris Flannery
JV Fox
Wolfgang Freudenmann
John Gee
Iona Gibson
Mr and Mrs R Gilmore
N Godfrey
Mrs V Gorst
Peter Green
Joy Hatwood
Councillor
    Gerry Harrison
Sir Derek Jacobi

Councillor Ernest James
Derek Kelley
Mr JK Killby
Mrs RL Klausner
Roland & Frederika
    Kommerell
Mrs Rita Krier-Wolf
Andrew Lawrence
Clive Leverton
Mrs D Lewin
Mr N Lion
Gordon MacLean
James Mallinson
Helen Marcus
Harold Marks
Max and Judy Nasatyr
Masihiro Nomura
Mrs A Nottman

Mrs A Obholzer
Jonathan Pritchard
Pru Rex-Hassan
EK Roberts
Mrs Ellen Schmidt
Stephen Schneider
Sir Michael Schofield
Diana Self
Dr Alan Selwyn
Mary Shenal
Adrian Shire
Joy Silver
Baron Sleigh
    of Carbury
Dr Peter Smith
WG Solomon
BC Southgate
Lady Mary Stirling

Kathryn Stubbs
T Tipping
Gwen Thorstad
DS Unwin
Mrs Williams
Anthony Wills
AM Wilson
Sheila Wilson
Joan Wilton
Mrs B Wober
Anthony and
    Susan Wright
Noel Wurr
Benny and
    Deirdre Yager

PREFACE

In 1986, the Belsize Conservation Area Advisory Committee held an exhibition of photographs entitled *Belsize: a living suburb*, and published a book under the same name. (This is not what the BCAAC usually does: that is explained at the back of this book.) Now, this millennium year has prompted the Committee to revive, bring up to date and expand both the exhibition and the book. The present edition includes all the original articles and adds a number of new ones, roughly doubling its size.

The exhibition and book provide a permanent record of some of the fine buildings and distinctive streets of this part of Belsize. The authors of the book all are (or were) local people with a deep love and knowledge of Belsize, and they include some distinguished architects and historians.

Belsize lacked the cachet of Hampstead, Primrose Hill or St John's Wood, and the rowdy energy of Camden Town. The original exhibition could therefore be seen in part as an act of assertiveness.

It was also a celebration of a group of mostly nineteenth-century streets that competently adapted to the twentieth, have survived intact to a remarkable degree and have accommodated modern and often shoddy incursions with some dignity.

The central purpose of the original exhibition, however, was to stimulate and broaden interest in conservation. The conservation movement was less established then, and rising housing prices increased the threat of insensitive 'development', or worse.

It might be argued that the fabric of Belsize is more secure fourteen years later, but, as several expert authors argue here, much of it is still under threat from mean-spirited or ignorant adaptation and neglect.

There is a debate, though, which is reflected here. So much of the post-war building in Belsize has damaged the townscape, or at least failed to enhance it, that it is tempting to regard a stern regime of preservation and rehabilitation as the only choice. We celebrate successful acts of restoration – most recently that of Hampstead Town Hall – and we fight to present further damage being done, but this book also describes some of the better contemporary buildings in the neighbourhood. Not all change is for the worse.

Of course, terms like 'historical' and 'modern', and the question of what should be conserved, depend on where you happen to be standing at the time. A section of this book is devoted to Isokon, a block of flats built in 1933-34 in Lawn Road. A ground-breaking modernist building in its time, but sadly neglected of late, it has acquired a strong band of supporters who are fighting for it to be restored. As we write, its future is in the balance.

And so, too, is that of many buildings, some of them as important as Isokon, but mostly modest and domestic in

Adrian Shire

scale. It is instructive to be reminded by our authors that in historical terms Belsize is actually quite a modern suburb: most of the streets were first laid out between 1850 and the first world war. Before the buildings that we see now, there was a Belsize that was swept away, of which almost nothing remains. It can happen again.

Belsize in 1963, seen from the south-east. Haverstock Hill is at the top, St Dominic's Priory lower right, with Parkhill Road just behind it. AEROFILMS LTD

Introduction

CHANGING ATTITUDES TO CONSERVATION

A personal view

It is fourteen years since the Belsize Conservation Area Advisory Committee mounted the photographic exhibition 'Belsize: a living suburb', and published the original edition of this book under the same name. At the time this was a bold and brave move to raise public awareness of the character of the area, to warn of the threats to the subtle qualities which form that character, and to be a rallying cry for vigilance and action in the face of unwelcome changes. Fourteen years on, what has changed, and what has remained resolutely the same?

Globally, one can say that conservation in its broadest sense has come of age. Green political parties have become a serious force at the ballot box, while environmental pressure groups such as Greenpeace and Friends of the Earth are having to adjust their agendas because many of the arguments have been won. Global warming is no longer seen as a crackpot theory promulgated by scaremongers. Climate change is now a fact of life, even if nothing very effective is yet being done to arrest it. Green issues are regularly discussed in the media, in schools, in pubs and in churches. The public outcry against genetic modification of foodstuffs and the burgeoning demand for organically grown produce illustrate this increasing awareness and concern.

There is also a greater public interest than ever before in the conservation of the built environment. The designation of World Heritage Sites and the parallel growth of the tourist trade and the 'Heritage Industry' result in more and more of us travelling further and further and more and more often, to flock into historic towns, palaces, parks, cathedrals, museums and so on. All of this travel is, of course, decidedly un-green, but flagship historic buildings and sites are now definitely big business. Just as happens with vulnerable sites of outstanding natural beauty, of course, mass tourism also brings with it real risks of destroying the very qualities which attracted people in the first place. Belsize Park is mercifully free of 'honeypots' that attract visitors in such numbers. Up the hill in Hampstead, though, one wonders how many more young people can possibly cram in on summer weekends, and how many more traditional pubs will succumb to conversion to café-bars in the effort to part them from their money.

Nationally, the concept of the conservation of historic buildings has become the accepted norm. Over the last

I H Stewart

"...traditional pubs..."; the Load of Hay, Haverstock Hill (1863).

PHOTOGRAPH BY IH STEWART

fourteen years, the control system and its legislative framework have been consolidated, with re-surveys of the listed building stock, designation of more conservation areas, endless Planning Policy Guidance Notes from central government amongst other measures enshrining the place of archaeology in redevelopment proposals, the appointment of conservation officers by larger local authorities such as Camden, and the ever wider consultation with amenity groups. The presumption now is definitely in favour of retaining and enhancing historic buildings, whereas the emphasis in the past, in the face of development proposals, was that their retention would have to be justified by argument.

Control systems are a two-edged weapon, of course. We applaud them when they frustrate the other man's utterly inappropriate and ill-conceived proposals, but when our own tasteful, uncontentious, wholly benign schemes meet with delays, nit-picking criticisms or ill-informed obstruc-

tion from self-appointed busybodies who have not even taken the trouble to understand the submission in detail – that is a different matter! There is a genuine danger of reaction against planning and listed building controls that are perceived as becoming Draconian or Byzantine. Our planning laws are set up, not to initiate action, but to react to submissions made by building owners, developers and their architects. In the best cases, a creative dialogue develops, but it is always too easy for an ill-informed, badly trained or just plain overworked officer to say 'no'. This gives rise to resentment, and ultimately discredits the system.

One must also keep a very clear perspective on the role of the amenity societies and other consultees in the planning process. Of course public consultation and canvassing for opinions is right and proper. The public expects and deserves no less. However, the more opinions are gathered, the less consensus there is likely to be. Ultimately, someone has to evaluate those opinions, and make a decision based on information and not on prejudice. There are five statutory amenity societies which are consulted on listed building consent applications – the Society for the Protection of Ancient Buildings, the Ancient Monuments Society, the Georgian Group, The Victorian Society and the 20th Century Society. All started life as pressure groups, to a greater or lesser extent, and, quite legitimately, each has its own particular axe to grind. Although the committees of these bodies may be elected by the membership, they are essentially unrepresentative and unaccountable. Likewise, the Officers of English Heritage, who consider cases both for statutory control and for possible grant aid, are mandated only by appointed committees.

Grant aid for the conservation and repair of historic buildings is another area which has an enormous influence, and which has undergone major change through the

St Peter's Belsize Square is one of the Belsize buildings that has benefited from the availability of grants.

PHOTOGRAPH BY
IH STEWART

Worship. This scheme is now heavily oversubscribed, having vastly increased its remit to include buildings of all faiths and denominations, whether listed Grade I, II* or II, and even unlisted buildings in Conservation Areas. Last year's round of applications had a total value of more than five times the available grant budget. Consequently the goalposts went on the move again, and all manner of relatively arbitrary criteria were introduced to limit eligibility. St Peter's Church, Belsize Park, was extremely fortunate to attract one of these grants.

Like it or not, the Lottery is a fact of life now, but the distribution of its funds needs more radical rethinking if it is to develop its potential for enhancing the built environment. Vast investments in very high-profile projects such as the Millennium Dome and the Royal Opera House have understandably given rise to great resentment and criticism. If the folk who buy the Lottery tickets are going to see some tangible benefits in the enhancement of their own local environment, a much simpler, grass-roots method of distribution has to be devised. Local authorities are empowered to make grants of up to 50% of the cost of repair and maintenance of historic buildings and their gardens. They can also offer interest-free loans. In practice, very few authorities have a budget of any significance from which to make such offers. Maybe block grants from the Lottery could revive this scheme in a way that could be seen really to benefit localities such as Belsize Park.

Another area where real assistance could be given would be in the reform of the VAT rules. Sadly there has been no change whatever over the past fourteen years in the anomaly by which approved alterations to listed buildings in non-business use can be zero-rated for VAT, yet all repairs and maintenance work attract the full tax. For years, concerned groups have been lobbying to reverse this situation, or, if that was too unpalatable to our own government or the EU, at least to establish a uniform,

emergence of the National Lottery, in the shape of the Heritage Lottery Fund. When the Lottery started, the rhetoric was that it would generate new money for 'good causes', and existing funding would be unaffected. With the passage of time, it seems that a different reality is emerging. Take the area that I know well in the repair of historic churches. Before the Lottery there was a well established if slightly long-winded system of grant aid from English Heritage. After the introduction of the Lottery, less and less assistance from English Heritage has seemed to be available, with many applications being referred to the Heritage Lottery Fund, whose own application procedures were so complex and the goalposts of whose criteria for eligibility were so mobile, that getting a grant offer really was a lottery. The confusion was eventually reduced by subsuming both grant schemes in the Joint Grant Scheme for Churches and Other Places of

Left: "…parking schemes, traffic-calming measures, lights, signs, railings and an increasing display of road paints and surfaces".

Right: "a multitude of equipment cabinets".

PHOTOGRAPHS BY JH STEWART

reduced rate for all building work. The pleas still fall on deaf ears, even though the effect of such a simple change could enormously benefit our building stock as a whole, and quite probably employment prospects in the building industry as well.

So what noticeable effect have these global and national developments had locally? One has to conclude that there has been precious little. That, however, can be interpreted as a good thing. As I said at the outset, the original exhibition and publication of the book were seen as a response to a perceived threat to the area. If that threat has not been fulfilled in the change and erosion of the character of the area, that must be at least partly attributable to a generally greater awareness of and belief in conservation values. The book and exhibition must have contributed to that awareness in no small measure.

While the positive side of 'no change' is that we can still enjoy the buildings and vistas of our tree-lined streets,

there has to be a negative side as well. We still suffer from the less appealing aspects of the locality, most of which have to do with the all-pervading motorcar and measures to curb it with parking schemes, traffic-calming measures, lights, signs, railings and an increasing Technicolor display of road paints and surfaces. All these bits of street furniture, gradually, inexorably and almost imperceptibly introduced by the traffic engineers (with all the best intentions), cumulatively have an enormous visual impact, and constitute one of the most obvious differences when one compares a photograph of even twenty years ago with the present view. Also included in this catalogue of street clutter is the multitude of equipment cabinets for telecommunications and cable TV. Quite substantial boxes appear down every street, often conspicuously and obstructively sited, without any consultation or apparent planning constraints. We also still suffer the effects of the 'school run', to the extent

PHOTOGRAPH BY IH STEWART

The well restored façade of 15 Lancaster Grove enhances the building, the street and the neighbourhood. The contrast with its neighbours on either side bears witness to the value of property conservation.

that this area was singled out in a recent report for Radio 4's *Today* programme.

So far as individual buildings go, there have been successes and failures in about equal numbers, and some enduring causes célèbres have yet to be resolved. The Town Hall has been sumptuously restored, the Lyndhurst Road Chapel has a beneficial use as a recording studio, while St Stephen's church opposite on Rosslyn Hill still stands empty (although its future now at last seems assured). We have lost 15 Eton Avenue, the future of the Isokon flats in Lawn Road remains uncertain and the Swiss Cottage development at the edge of our area is again in the melting pot.

This last case seems to me to illustrate some of the dilemmas which arise from the changing attitudes to conservation and the ascendancy of the heritage lobby. The recent round of listing twentieth-century buildings has produced some very odd choices. There seems to be a loss of confidence and lack of judgement about what buildings really are good and deserve saving. The easy option is to play safe and save everything, but if earlier generations had adopted that attitude we would never have had half the outstanding buildings that we now value and protect with listed status. The danger of the 'dead hand' of protection is that it will generate a backlash and set back the whole cause of conservation. Are the Basil Spence buildings at Swiss Cottage that good? Do they function adequately, and are they affordable to maintain? One effect of Heritage Lottery Fund grant conditions, although it seems initially to be just another bureaucratic delaying tactic, might in the long run be of great value, and that is the production of a Conservation Plan. The purpose of this document is to assess objectively the significance or heritage merit of a building or site, and how that significance is vulnerable or sensitive to change, and to define policies for retaining or enhancing the significance. This approach could be a useful way of sifting the special pleadings of single-interest amenity groups, the business lobby and so on. With a few notable exceptions, we are not as bold or inventive as most of our continental neighbours at marrying really first-rate

Handsome and well restored, this neo-classical portico is a credit to its owner and the craftsmen who have worked on it.

PHOTOGRAPH BY IH STEWART

modern design with an historic environment. Quality will always sit happily with quality.

Excellence of design, whether of new work or conservation of old, requires both inspiration and adequate training. Training alone will not do. It can develop competence, but not excellence. A great deal more training is available now for conservation practitioners – architects, surveyors, conservators, builders and craftsmen of all sorts. Conservation has become an academic discipline; degree courses and diplomas abound. All this competence is obviously a good thing, and is increasingly being measured by accreditation schemes. These seem to me to be of little value, however. You can test competence, up to a point, but you cannot test inspiration: that can only be demonstrated by track record. I liken the way that the conservation world is developing to the evolution of the Gothic revival in the nineteenth century. In the early years, 'gothick' was a style you could apply eclectically as an

alternative to classical motifs. Many well-proportioned, handsome, charming buildings resulted. As the century moved on, the whole study of mediaeval architecture became a serious academic and moral pursuit, and the resulting buildings became altogether more serious. In the hands of a few masters – Pugin, Street, Butterfield, Pearson – they could be inspirational. In the hands of the majority of lesser designers, they were competent but deadly dull. The fun had gone out of the work. We are in danger of losing the fun of working with old buildings now.

Finally I should like to explode the myth that you cannot get the craftsmen these days to match the old work. Craftsmen are available in all trades, if you know where to look, and we have a duty to look, so as to ensure that these skills are retained and developed. There is training, as mentioned above, and, ironically, major disasters over recent years, such as the fires at York Minster, Hampton Court Palace, Uppark and Windsor Castle, have done a great deal to foster craft skills during the reinstatement projects. However, quality must be paid for. Sadly, the allegedly cheaper cowboy builder will always be with us, because owners of unlisted historic buildings in areas such as Belsize Park, who cannot attract grant aid, will always think they can get a better deal. In the long run, this better deal almost always proves to be an illusion. Inappropriate materials, inadequate preparation, poor workmanship: none will last, and all can lead to more serious consequential defects, which will cost a great deal more to remedy. This is another thing that has not changed, as you will see from Leon Krier's article, reprinted here from that first edition of fourteen years ago.

HOPE SPRINGS ETERNAL

A *few thoughts on Belsize Park*

This comment is generated more by questions than by answers. The starting point lay in asking what relevance had the designation of specific conservation areas to the sustenance and quality of urban environment over the whole of an interlocked neighbourhood – that diffuse, ill-defined area lying between Hampstead proper, Chalk Farm, Finchley Road and Kentish Town, and called, not without an occasional touch of the pejorative, Belsize Park. Is there in any comprehensible terms a plan for its future? Do development, change and replacement take place within a clearly articulated concept, or are they to be the result of speculative pressures, curbed only by confused, statistically based planning control? Is this primarily residential network of streets to remain in such use? Or is a gradual transformation to take place, with associated increase in density? Local community groups may oppose such a trend, but will protestations be seen as unrealistic and sentimental in face of the 'necessary thrusting growth' of the metropolis?

For a condensed, well researched summary of the history, growth, origins and physical presence of Belsize Park there is no better source than the stream of publications published by the Camden History Society. These are edited and some are written by Christopher Wade. The 1973 booklet *More Streets of Hampstead* (now long out of print) subsumes Belsize Park within Hampstead, and the emergent 'Belsize Park' identity receives short shrift. The later publication *The Streets of Belsize* (1991, still available) concedes the right to an individual identity.

However, each person constitutes a filter through which the area takes on different forms, the perceptions varying according to where they live relative to the spinal cord of Haverstock Hill. The Eton Estate, for example, would be regarded by some as 'only just' Belsize Park. This was tacitly recognised by the residents who demanded and obtained a conservation area advisory committee of their own. Even more so South End Green, despite its close links and common causes with Belsize Park groups, has its own very clear individual territory, with a well organised community. Another unambiguous physical and psychological boundary is where Elsworthy Road meets Avenue Road.

More or less unknown is the delightful group of buildings constituting the St Pancras Almshouses. These are not visible from Belsize Park, but they lie within the Upper Park Road / Parkhill / Lawn Road Conservation Area.

To the north, the limits are clearly and monumentally set by Samuel Sanders Teulon's St Stephen's at the top of Pond Street. The long, gross neglect of this fine building is

Jake Brown

Editor's note: This is a revised version of an article that appeared in the 1986 edition of this book.

The St Pancras Almshouses (1852–62) in Southampton Road.

PHOTOGRAPH BY
MARY SHENAI

a local and national disgrace. At the time of writing there is a glimmer of hope that part of the local community, in the form of an adjacent school, may, with the aid of Lottery money, be able to restore it for an appropriate use.

Only a stone's throw beyond are a number of splendid houses for 'gentlemen artists' in Hampstead Hill Gardens. Batterbury and Huxley, the architects, are also represented by several houses in Steele's Road, again for artists, and distinguished by the use of 'Queen Anne' motifs.

Wherever and at what time the amorphous content of Belsize Park is fixed must be a parochial consideration, however, and the primary questions remain to be asked.

Firstly, what are the characteristics of Belsize Park which argue for retention and for a particular sensitivity to change? Secondly, has Belsize Park an identity of its own, and, if so, how is the existing or emerging community able to participate in and monitor the many and accumulating pressures on its environment?

In its favour, Belsize Park has an overall domestic scale, with a sufficiency of substantial villas all built within a period of forty or so years to provide a strong urban form. Generous gardens still abound, despite the inroads of development, and an abundance of trees includes many mature forest specimens. A rich selection of Edwardian and eclectic styles of architecture provides a foil for the dominance of stucco semi-detached Italianate villas. These in themselves run the whole gamut of Greek and Roman and Renaissance influences, with all the ingenuity and variety of the pattern-book building of Victorian development. Mews and backwaters abound. Haverstock Hill itself, due to the building line set by a never realised road widening, enjoys pavements of considerable gener-osity, giving a sense of focus and place not wholly different from that of a village green or a small town market street.

The area generally is vulnerable to over-develop-ment and a steady erosion of architectural quality by

Belsize Grove.

PHOTOGRAPH BY
JAKE BROWN

opportunist and ill-considered additive work. Despite planning control and monitoring by conservation groups, there is clear evidence of impoverishment of much of the building fabric.

It is in the nature of the stucco facades that a major part of the architectural expression is little more than skin deep, and consequently reliant on sustained, conscientious maintenance. The surface and mouldings of such houses can literally disintegrate and drop off, leaving them exposed to crude, barebones economic repairs which diminish these houses, sometimes beyond recall. Chimney stacks, gateposts, boundary walls, steps and guard-rails, as well as the proportional systems, are essential and functional components of the architectural vocabulary. All these features are early casualties in the many conversions and adaptations to which the houses are inevitably subject.

The second question – that of identity – is even less easily answered. The Belsize Village group of streets has a vigorous residents' association. Otherwise the whole community has only come together and 'waxed and waned' in response to particular planning issues. Perhaps one of the most deeply felt expression of collective opinion was the attempt to persuade Camden to retain a relaxed public amenity side by side with a modest provision of new housing on the Russell Nurseries site. This relatively unknown backwater had the Globe Tennis Club in partial occupation, with a tiny but unspoilt remnant of wood and hedgerows. This could have been developed as a civic 'wild park', directly accessible from the heart of shopping and transport facilities. This idea did not carry the day. A similar long struggle over land use at Swiss Cottage, where the arguments were parallel, also proved to be a lost cause. At the time of writing, even more dense development, despite resistance, is forging ahead. A positive blessing was the development which included the Screen on the Hill cinema. The scale and treatment of the new building was handled with skill and sensitivity, giving a valuable cultural focus to the locality.

Since the foregoing text was written in 1986 there have been emphatic changes. The stream of traffic congestion on Haverstock Hill has reached crisis levels. Widespread parking controls have improved conditions in local roads, although acute reduction of usable widths is common-place. Speed humps (long awaited) are coming to many places. The broad pavements related to the shops and Tube station on Haverstock Hill are now thronged with restaurants and outside seating reminiscent of continental cities. The pavements are unimaginatively finished, dirty, unkempt and in general unworthy of this intense social ambience. The reconstituted and extended Town Hall is a major step forward in civic provision – but can we look forward to easy access for the community (now a much weakened and elusive creature)? Does the community exist, even? In what sense is the suburb 'living'? and can it begin to look after itself?

The recently arrived flocks of screeching, raucous, wheeling seagulls which now haunt Belsize Park may offer a clue. Are they laughing, or crying?

BELSIZE HOUSE

In AD 986, King Ethelred the Unready granted the manor of Hampstead to the Abbot of Westminster. Part of the territory later became the manor of Belsize (originally Bel Assis: 'pleasantly situated'). Early in the fourteenth century it was to be found in the hands of Sir Roger le Brabazon, Lord Chief Justice to Edward II. On his deathbed in 1317, however, he restored the house and fifty-seven acres to the Abbot and Convent of Westminster.

Modern Belsize is mostly the western part of this later manor, which also included land on the east side of Haverstock Hill, between Downside Crescent and the parish boundary south of the Load of Hay public house. Much of the rest of our area, south of England's Lane, Lambolle Place and (roughly) Lancaster Grove, lies in the Eton College estate, also called the Chalcots estate. This originated in a grant, in or before the twelfth century, of Hampstead land to the Hospital of St James for leprous women in London, which in turn was placed under the College by Henry VI. England's Lane, somewhat longer than at present, led to the main farm on the estate, Upper Chalcots. Ethelred's manor of Hampstead, reduced in size, and in lay hands since 1551, contributes part of Belsize Lane and of the east side of Haverstock Hill, down to just past the tube station.

By the middle of the sixteenth century, the Belsize estate consisted of a number of farms and an important manor house, at the very edge of its manor. Little is known of the early versions of this house, but it seems likely that one was built in 1496, when Westminster ordered 400,000 bricks in Belsize. They were probably made in Brick Field, above the Belsize Tavern. In 1568 the house had 24 rooms, including a hall, long gallery and great chamber.

In 1542, after the dissolution of the monasteries, Henry VIII returned the estate once more to the newly constituted Dean and Chapter of Westminster. From 1557, the lease was held by Armigell Waad, or Wade, Clerk of the Council to Henry VIII and Edward VI. He studied for the bar, and after a voyage to Newfoundland in 1536, was known as 'the English Columbus', albeit with little justification. He was nevertheless a notable traveller; in 1540 he became Clerk to the Council of Calais, then still an English possession, and in 1559 he led a mission to the Duke of Holstein.

Waad died at Belsize in 1568, and was buried in the old Hampstead parish church. The manor passed to his son, William, born 1546, who, like his father, studied law and served Lord Burghley in France and Italy, and became Clerk of the Council under Elizabeth and James I.

William Waad was employed on difficult missions, the most delicate being to Philip of Spain in 1584. Elizabeth had expelled the Spanish ambassador, Mendoza,

Roy Allen

Editor's note: Parts of this article appeared in the 1986 edition of this book.

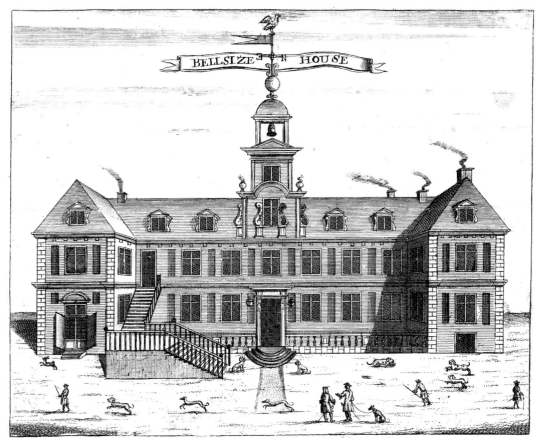

The version of Belsize House built in 1663, in an engraving of about 1780.

CAMDEN LOCAL STUDIES AND ARCHIVE CENTRE

and Waad was sent to disclose to the king full details of Mendoza's conduct. Philip, who had secretly decided on invasion, declined to give him an audience, referring him to the royal council; Waad refused to deal with them and returned home. The stage was set for the Armada.

Back from Spain, Waad took part in negotiations with Mary, Queen of Scots, then imprisoned at Sheffield. Two years later, it was he who seized the papers that implicated Mary in the Babington plot. Elizabeth excused him from attending Mary's execution.

Sir William (he was knighted by James I) spent his last years at Belsize and at his estate in Essex, where he died in 1623. Anne, his widow, married Colonel Thomas Bushell. On the outbreak of the Civil War in 1642, they put up Belsize as security for a loan from Serjeant Wilde, a neighbour and parliamentarian, although the money was apparently needed to equip Bushell for service in the Royalist army.

In 1661, after the Restoration, the Dean and Chapter of Westminster ignored Bushell's claim to the estate and granted the next lease to another Royalist veteran, Colonel

Daniel O'Neill. Two years later, O'Neill became the third husband of Katherine, Lady Stanhope; she had been active for the King during the Commonwealth and had recently been created Countess of Chesterfield.

Apparently also in 1663, O'Neill started building the historic version of Belsize House, the first for which there are illustrations. This was a typical Restoration mansion, with projecting wings and a central tower. With a frontage of 120 feet, it lay astride Belsize Park (the street) between St Peter's Church and the crossroads below Belsize Village, facing Haverstock Hill up a long drive which is now Belsize Avenue. The house and its twenty-five acres of gardens and park were enclosed in a 1,400-yard pentagonal wall, of which the north-east side is reflected in the angle of Belsize Park Gardens, and the south side in a wall between Lancaster Grove and Crossfield Road.

O'Neill died in 1664, before the house was finished, and on Katherine's death in 1667 the lease passed to Henry Kirkhoven, Lord Wotton, her son by her second husband. Wotton was here until 1682. He greatly improved the gardens, and also farmed some twenty-six of the fifty-eight acres of demesne land, along Belsize Lane, including Brick Field. Pepys, who visited the house in 1668, wrote that the gardens were "wondrous fine" but "too good for the house". Evelyn, visiting the house some years later, described them as "very large but ill-kept, yet woody and chargeable; the soil a cold, weeping clay".

Local history owes much to Wotton, for he commissioned from William Gent the first large-scale map of Belsize (then amounting to 235 acres); it also included his other holding, the Manor of St John's Wood, which met Belsize at College Crescent. Gent's map, dated 1679, shows that, on rising ground in Belsize Village, there was a "water house" which would have drawn supplies, probably in wooden pipes, from the manor pond on Rosslyn Hill, below Thurlow Road. Further pipes may have led to parts of the mansion, but drinking water would have been fetched (or delivered by carrier) from the Shepherd's Well, near the junction of Fitzjohn's Avenue and Akenside Road. Gent also shows the kitchen garden, up against the south-east wall beyond the park.

Wotton was the last tenant to act as lord of the manor, and on his death the estate went to Philip Stanhope, Katherine's son by her first husband, and now second Earl of Chesterfield. He and the later earls did not reside locally, the mansion and demesne land being sub-let. One privilege remained, however: the manor pond, although over 500 yards outside the grounds, still belonged to whoever occupied Belsize House.

In the early 1700s, Charles Povey was the sub-tenant of Belsize and the twenty-five acres enclosed by the wall. He seems to have been a character both ambitious and none too scrupulous, an author, pamphleteer, inventor, and founder of the Sun Fire Office. At one point he had entered the coal trade, where, being harassed by the established merchants, he published a *Discovery* of their 'Indirect Practices'. In 1709, he incurred the wrath of the Postmaster-General by launching a halfpenny letter post service in London, Westminster and Southwark, a venture that ended in a £100 fine for infringement of monopoly.

Povey renamed the place The Wilderness, and introduced deer hunts in the park, and other events. In 1710, he built Sion Chapel for easy marriages, where any couple with the necessary licence might be married for a fee of only five shillings, provided the wedding breakfast was held in the grounds. Suspicions arose that the requirement for the licence might on occasion be overlooked, but the chapel was still functioning in 1716. John Grove's map of 1714 suggests that it was near 22 Belsize Park. Povey tried (in vain) to make a virtue of having refused to let the house to the French ambassador, who wanted the chapel for Roman Catholic services.

In 1720, Povey sub-let The Wilderness to James Howell,

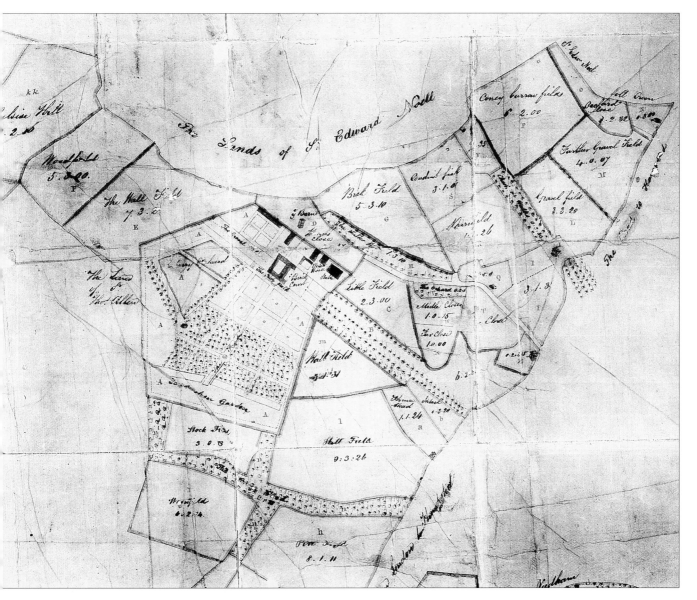

William Gent's map of 1679.

CAMDEN LOCAL STUDIES AND ARCHIVE CENTRE

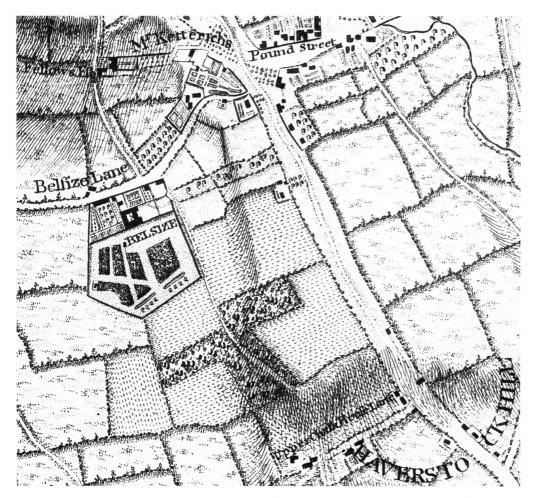

A detail from John Rocque's map of Belsize dated 1746, showing the distinctive pentagon of the Belsize House estate.

CAMDEN LOCAL STUDIES AND ARCHIVE CENTRE

who changed the name back to Belsize House, but there was still a wilderness, where the birds put up a morning chorus of "pleasant harmony". Howell, who for some reason soon became known as the Welsh Ambassador, saw no future in weddings, threw the place open to the public and set out to rival Vauxhall in the attractions on offer. House and grounds were open from six in the morning until eight at night, and indoors there were concerts and informal music, dancing in a lavishly furnished ballroom, and drinking and dining. Deer continued to be hunted in the park, and an occasional fox; in 1722 a deer hunt attracted three or four hundred coaches. There were also horse races and foot races. Twelve "stout fellows", later increased to thirty, escorted customers back to London.

The high point was a visit in 1721 by the Prince and Princess of Wales. But a reputation for doubtful

The southernmost remnant of the footpath that ran from Hampstead to England's lane. A little to the south it became Cut-Throat Alley. PHOTOGRAPH BY MARY SHENAI

The southernmost remnant of the footpath that ran from Hampstead to England's lane. A little to the south it became Cut-Throat Alley. PHOTOGRAPH BY MARY SHENAI

social contacts, for which there was ample opportunity, began to tell, and in 1722 Belsize was described in verse as a "scandalous lewd house". Gambling crept in, too, and this led to a police raid, in which Howell was arrested, along with some "common Gamesters". He was held in Newgate Prison, but released on a writ of Habeas Corpus.

Faced with a decline in fashionable visitors, Howell set aside part of the house for customers of the "meaner sort". This was on the north side of the building, but an outside staircase on the main front suggests that on the first floor there was further accommodation for the common people. In the end the authorities closed the house itself, although events continued in the park; a foot race was held there as late as 1745.

The landscape around the estate was still rural, but the

The Cottage formerly Sir Rich. Steele's, Haverstock Hill.

last of the woodland vanished in the 18th century. A striking avenue of Spanish chestnuts led from opposite Pond Street to Rosslyn House, behind numbers 26 and 27 Lyndhurst Road (the large old stump facing number 28 Lyndhurst Gardens appears to be a relic). The main road had wide verges, and there were well-used footpaths. One long one ran from Church Row in Hampstead to England's Lane, part of it surviving in Spring Path (off Fitzjohn's Avenue) and in the passage from Lyndhurst Gardens to Belsize Place. After crossing the future village, it ran down the north-east wall of the park, where, one hopes fancifully, it was known as Cut-Throat Alley.

The fields, irregular in shape, averaged about five acres north of Belsize Lane. Lower down, some were larger; there was one of 16 acres west of England's Lane. The plough had long been disappearing, however, and by 1800 there was only one still at work, around Adamson and Winchester Roads. All the rest of Belsize was pasture and meadow. (This is vouched for by Washington Irving, who

"All the rest of Belsize was pasture and meadow." An engraving of Steele's Cottage in 1818. In the distance can be seen St Paul's.

Left: The 1745 version of Belsize House, shown in an engraving of 1800, when Spencer Perceval was the tenant. CAMDEN LOCAL STUDIES AND ARCHIVE CENTRE

Above: Belsize Lodge, gatehouse to Belsize House, in about 1845. WATERCOLOUR BY COURTESY OF ROY ALLEN

stayed for a while at Steele's Cottage on Haverstock Hill. In *Tales of a Traveller* (1824), he recalls that haymaking distracted his thoughts while he was trying to write. The haymakers, mostly Irish, found it thirsty work, but opposite the cottage was the appropriately named Load of Hay.) There were ponds everywhere, in fields and by the roadside, the largest being the manor pond, nearly half an acre in extent.

By 1746, Howell had departed and Belsize had been rebuilt, by one Joshua Evans, and become a residence again: a plain Georgian mansion, with a short extension set back to the right. This at first sight seems to be a completely new house, but it might be the result of adding a Georgian front, one room deep, to the south-east side of the old building, while demolishing the parts no longer required. The extension to the right would then have been the left-hand projecting wing of the historic mansion, with an extra storey added to match the new roof line. The house now faced London. From 1797 it was occupied by Spencer Perceval until he became Prime Minister in 1809;

in 1812 he was assassinated in the House of Commons. He is commemorated in the nearby Perceval Avenue. He made some improvements, but his family appears to have preferred their town house in Lincoln's Inn Fields.

In 1807, the fifth Earl of Chesterfield sold the head lease of the manor to a syndicate of local men, with the result that Belsize House and forty-five acres were now held direct from the Dean and Chapter of Westminster. Then, probably in 1811–12, the last version of the house was built, this time on the other side of the crossroads. It again faced Haverstock Hill, with the main front straddling Belsize Avenue alongside number 10.

Later again, the name of the house was changed to Belsize Park, perhaps because 11 Rosslyn Hill (which still stands) was calling itself Belsize. The change may have been made by John Wright, leading light of Wright & Co., a private family bank. He arrived in 1824 or 1825, and bought much local property, including (in 1830) the head lease of his own house. This all came to a sudden end in 1840 with the failure of the bank, said to be

The last version of Belsize House, in an engraving of 1845; it was to be demolished eight years later.

CAMDEN LOCAL STUDIES AND ARCHIVE CENTRE

due largely to his "extraordinary mania" for the "most adventurous speculations". During his time, an unknown artist painted watercolours of the main front and entrance on Haverstock Hill.

In 1841 the house was taken over by a wine merchant, Sebastian Gonzalez Martinez. He kept the name Belsize Park, and set up a toll for horses and carriages in the private part of Belsize Lane, with a gate just west of Daleham Mews. Queen Victoria, on her way to consider Rosslyn House as a possible holiday home for her children, is said to have been called upon to pay toll by a small girl who had been left in charge of the gate. A likely time for this incident was the summer of 1853, and the girl could have been Eliza White, the eight-year-old daughter of the gatekeeper.

Martinez departed in 1852, the house reverted to its historic name, and it was demolished in the autumn of 1853 to make way for new housing. About six yards of the ancient wall survives, and may be glimpsed end-on between 14 and 16 Belsize Avenue. Creeper usually covers most of this relic, but there is a distant view of the whole length, with a large pillar on the right, from between 9 and 11 Belsize Park Gardens. It may have been realigned early in the 19th century, but it remains one of the oldest structures in Belsize.

BIBLIOGRAPHY

Dictionary of National Biography
Victoria County History, Middlesex IX (1989), I
The Annals of Hampstead, Thomas J Barratt, I, 1912, reprinted 1972
Hampstead One Thousand, John Richardson, 1985
Hampstead: Building a Borough, 1650–1964, FML Thompson, 1974

Above: Hunter's Lodge, Belsize Lane.

GLC ARCHITECTURAL DEPARTMENT

Left: A window of Crown Lodge, Haverstock Hill.

GLC ARCHITECTURAL DEPARTMENT

BELSIZE 1780–1870

Of Georgian Belsize there was never very much and now there is next to nothing. Precious for their antiquity and curiosity are these. Hunter's Lodge, Belsize Lane, is one of the two or three eighteenth-century *cottages ornées* still surviving in the London area. Another Georgian building of character, flanking Haverstock Hill, is stuccoed Crown Lodge. No less consequential historically are the post-Waterloo houses on what was the estate of Edward Bliss.

A group of three of stockbrick that have been beautifully restored line Haverstock Hill on its south-western side. Slightly higher up, in Belsize Grove, stands a neat terrace of stuccoed houses dating from the early eighteen-twenties, the survivors of a whole set built by individual owners on Bliss's land. Bliss, who for some obscure reason acquired the style and title of Baron Barreto in the Portuguese nobility, was the first developer to attract gentlemanly

Sir John Summerson

Editor's note: This article appeared in the 1986 edition of this book.

29

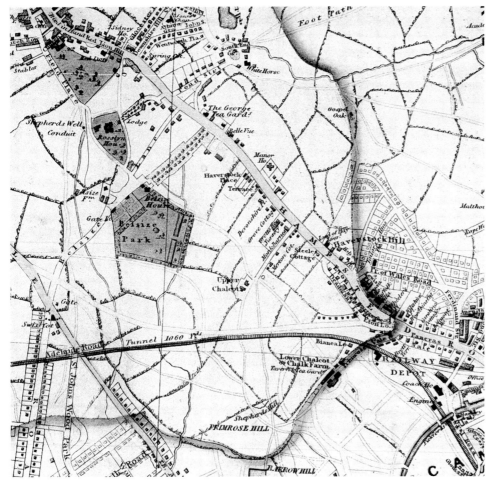

Belsize in 1848, in Wyld's map. The distinctive pentagram of the Belsize House estate persists, with its drive that became Belsize Avenue. The expanding encroachment of London is visible in St John's Wood and at the foot of Haverstock Hill.

CAMDEN LOCAL STUDIES AND ARCHIVE CENTRE

commuters to Haverstock Hill. Two other survivors – until a few months before this article was written – were No. 40 Belsize Grove (where Mr John Maples of the famous furniture store lived) and Oak Lodge on Haverstock Hill, an uncommonly handsome villa of 1826 – both just demolished by a twentieth-century developer. All these were the outposted forerunners of genteel Belsize, and it was twenty years before large-scale development caught up with them.

Queen Victoria's London started to move northward in the eighteen-forties. It advanced in a series of enterprising thrusts, readily distinguishable on the map. Two are of striking regularity. One of these is the parallelogram of streets on what was and still partly is the Chalcots estate of Eton College, between Chalk Farm on the east and Swiss Cottage on the west. The other is a similarly distinct parallelogram in the district round Belsize Square. These

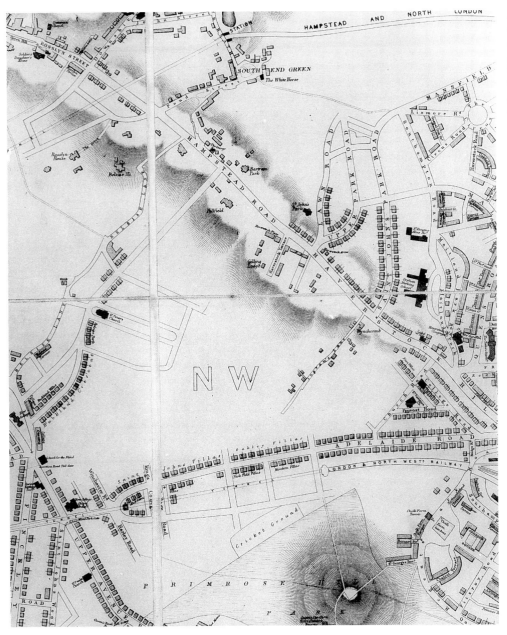

Belsize in 1862, mapped by Weller. The pentagonal Belsize House estate has faded away, but a vestige remains in the streets around Belsize Square.

CAMDEN LOCAL STUDIES AND ARCHIVE CENTRE

31

two symmetrical figures bear an absurd relationship to each other, like two logs colliding in a pond, a relationship eloquent of the way Victorian London developed, the old Georgian plan formula operating in two adjoining properties with blinkered indifference to each other. Then there is a third area, the former Haverstock Lodge estate, eastward of Haverstock Hill[1], which, if it strikes the eye at all, does so by the sheer nonsensical curvation of its streets. That is Victorian waywardness of another kind. Each of these three areas has its own colour, texture and architectural style, easily accounted for by the circumstances of their development.

Look first at the Eton College estate. The Provost and Fellows took little interest in their fields at Chalcots until in the eighteen-forties they were persuaded that they were sitting on what was, if not exactly a gold mine, a property of more value as building land than for grazing cattle. They instructed their excellent surveyor, John Shaw, to make a plan and advertise the letting of building leases. Which he did, creating the Eton parallelogram described, and extending it eventually beyond the newly dug railway cutting and tunnel to King Henry's Road.

1. Now the Parkhill Upper Park Road conservation area

9-10 Provost Road, with 'Choragic monument' window surrounds. GLC ARCHITECTURAL DEPARTMENT

The first builder to come on the scene was Samuel Cuming, a young carpenter from Devon. In 1843 he took a few sites at the east end of Adelaide Road, where some of his houses still stand. He disposed of them successfully, and went on to build the rows of villas in the triangular corner of the estate at Chalk Farm between Provost Road and Eton Road. He went on building on the estate until his death in 1870. The whole of Adelaide Road was his, and much of what lies north and south of it. He did very well, was elected a Hampstead vestry-man and left a comfortable annuity to his wife.

What of Cuming's architecture? His earliest houses are the best (as was mostly the case with Victorian developers), and they consist mainly of two types: square-cut, double-fronted detached houses, as in Adelaide Road; and semi-detached pairs of 'villas' with shared gables, as in the triangle round St Saviour's church. We do not know who designed them (not Cuming, surely; and Shaw merely approved them), but they are not without sophistication. They are 'school of John Nash', probably inspired by the assortment of villas Nash had designed for his own amusement at the Park Villages, Regents Park. In the Provost Road group it is, of course, the flattish gables with projecting eaves which authorise the epithet 'villa', evoking Italian vernacular virtues which, fifty years earlier, had been discovered with delight in the paintings of Claude. And Cuming's architect had an eye for 'the antique'. The stone caps of his gate piers are the lids of cinerary urns, and the surrounds to the ground floor windows are from a lost building of classical antiquity, the Choragic monument of Thrasyllos at Athens. If this latter derivation sounds a little far-fetched, let me assure the reader that in a popular builder's text-book of the eighteen-twenties the details of this monument are not only illustrated, but described as being "highly esteemed for their correct proportions and decided effect when carried into execution". In the higher reaches of the profession this sort of thing had been 'old hat' for twenty years, but to the suburban fringe it brought a nice augmentation of urbanity.

Now pass to the Belsize parallelogram. Here again the architecture seems to have been one man's doing (though again by the hand of an unnamed draughtsman). The developer was Daniel Tidey, who started building Buckland Crescent in 1856, went on to Belsize Square and then to the most memorable of his streets, Belsize Park Gardens, built in the fifties and early sixties. Tidey, who started as a bricklayer, was in a bigger way of business than Cuming, and speculated in South Kensington and Bayswater as well as Hampstead. He was concerned in the Boltons, on the Gunter estate, and in Bayswater built most if not all of Queens Gardens. What he was aiming to do at Belsize is fairly obvious. He was trying to attract custom by bringing the fashionable styles of the most showy western districts to the salubrious heights of the north.

By the fifties the fashionable styles had changed. The source of influence was no longer John Nash but Charles Barry – no longer 'the antique' but the Italian Renaissance.

Provost Road: "the stone caps of his gate piers are the lids of cinerary urns". PHOTOGRAPH BY MARY SHENAI

The Renaissance was found to be more robust, and there was the happy analogy of Victorian commercial prosperity with that of Florence under the Medici. Belsize Park Gardens is nothing if not robust. Everything is coarser and richer and bigger than Cuming's work. The balustrades, the columned porches, the rustic quoins and the full entablatures are of the Barry school; internally, the plaster cornices are grandly enriched and the hand-rails of the staircases are a massive handful. It is all very coarse and proud. Did it have the effect which Tidey desired? Mr Thompson, in his study of the area[2], seems to think not.

2. *F M L Thompson*, Hampstead: Building a Borough, 1650–1964.

The carriage class was not attracted, and the degree of affluence was of a more moderate kind, not above hiring horses and making the journey to town by cab or even omnibus. Tidey, moreover, overstretched himself and went bankrupt in 1870. In the 1881 census, as Roy Allen has discovered, Tidey, then aged 64, with his family, are stated as occupying the Belsize Tavern, the Belsize Village pub which he himself had built, presumably as the Landlord. The date of his death is unknown. 'Tideytown', as they called Belsize Village, is his monument[3].

It is interesting to compare Tidey's performance with Cuming's, both stylistically and socially. Cuming's houses, at the bottom of the hill, were taken by professional people of a modest sort, people in trade, solicitors, clergy, artists and literary men, but nobody of any real wealth. They had mostly one, sometimes two, servant girls living in. No men servants. I have not studied the census returns for Belsize Park Gardens, but I am pretty sure we should find more servants – look at those ample basements – and possibly a butler here and there. Stylistically, Belsize is more affluent than Chalk Farm, more essentially Victorian – and more philistine.

3. *In the following article, Mary Shenai talks in more detail about Daniel Tidey.*

This leaves us with the land developed by a Mr William Lund who lived at Haverstock Lodge, which stood where Downside Crescent now runs, and had a 99-year building lease from the ground landlords, the Dean and Chapter of Westminster. It does not appear that he employed a surveyor, and the curvaceous layout is perhaps his own idea. Mr Thompson tells us that Parkhill Road, Upper Park Road and Lawn Road follow the lines of the old field hedges, and their meanderings certainly give a picturesque aura to the district. The houses are architecturally less distinctive than either Cuming's or Tidey's. Both of them went in for stucco, while the houses on Lund's estate are brick with stucco ornaments, typical of thousands of middle-class houses in the inner suburbs of London in the eighteen-sixties. Richard Batterbury was the chief builder involved, and the architectural designs, one may guess, were concocted in his own office. The name Batterbury is a significant one in the architectural history of Hampstead. It was, I think, this builder's son who joined a Mr Huxley in an architectural partnership which raised a new standard of design in Hampstead, beginning with the artists' houses in Steele's Road and going on to the really distinguished collection of 'Queen Anne' in Hampstead Hill Gardens. But that is the beginning of another story which I leave the telling of to Mr Saint.

FASHION, FAMILY AND FORTUNE

Two builders in Belsize

Daniel Tidey

When Daniel Tidey arrived in Belsize in the late 1850s, his future seemed bright. Before him lay the acres of the park of the old Belsize House, run down and neglected, no doubt, but what matter, since he, Tidey, would shortly transform it into a vista of homes for middle-class gentlemen.

We who live there now are fortunate that, at a time when housing styles and fashions were changing rapidly between 1850 and 1900, land in Belsize became available at different times. Consequently, the houses in Belsize were not all built at the same time, and they reflect in miniature the dramatic changes in domestic building styles which were taking place throughout the country. Tidey was only one of the speculative builders who, taking advantage of the opening up of land around London to create new suburbs, propagated these changing styles.

By the 1850s there was already in architectural circles a strong trend away from the elegant classical styles of the eighteenth and early nineteenth centuries. The Gothic revival was under way: arches, round or pointed, in place of pediments, decorated brickwork in place of plain stucco, stained glass in place of clear, and more naturalistic decoration, all recalling Gothic church architecture, began to appear in the speculative builders' pattern books.

But Daniel Tidey would have none of this. His building career had already started in North Kensington and Chelsea, where he had taken part in building developments on the Grosvenor and Gunter estates. Here the east side of the crescent of the Boltons was largely built by him: large, stuccoed, semi-detached houses, with massive classical mouldings and proportions suggesting opulence. Surely Tidey must have been influenced by these when he came to plan his larger version of the Belsize Park houses. Similarly, his other pre-Belsize building operation, in Queen's Gardens, North Kensington, consists of a stuccoed terrace of basemented houses, with mouldings and enclosed porticoed entrances with side windows, which reappeared when he built Buckland Crescent.

Apart from two houses in College Crescent, Tidey's Belsize building began on the south side of Buckland Crescent. These are semi-detached houses with a half-basement, for there was already a move towards better domestic quarters, and Belsize Park afforded more space per house than Queen's Gardens. All the houses have

Mary Shenai

enclosed porticoes leading to a linear hall from which the stairs arise opposite the front door. But as he progresses along the street he begins to experiment with larger windows. On the first floor two of the three windows become one wider one, with one traditional upright one remaining over the porch. On the hall floor also, a wider single window appears next to the front door. (This had already been used in Queen's Gardens.) But it is only in the last two houses of Buckland Crescent that bay windows begin to appear, angled at the front and curved at the rear.

For Tidey was already preoccupied with the necessity of attracting purchasers, since financing had to be done on a hand-to-mouth basis. The move to larger windows was in general promoted by advances in glass technology, for which such buildings as Paxton's crystal palace and the Floral Hall at Covent Garden were the show-pieces, to say nothing of all the wonderful conservatories built for owners of large mansions. Having completed Buckland Crescent, Tidey introduced his piece de resistance in the magnificent curved glass rear bay windows of all his subsequent houses. With their recessed folding shutters and curved wrought iron balconies, these curved windows were, if not unique, at least unusual in speculative builders' houses, though they are seen in pattern books of larger individual villas of the time. Tidey was clearly aiming to go more upmarket. (See the note at the end of this article.) A contemporary advertisement offers them to let as "...a Noble Drawing room floor and kitchen" – presumably an anglicised version of the piano nobile.

After Buckland Crescent, Tidey settles for two main patterns for his houses, the slightly smaller ones of 1-16 Belsize Park and Belsize Square, and the larger ones of the remainder of Belsize Park and Belsize Park Gardens. The larger houses are distinguished externally by a different pattern of windows on the first floor under pedimented mouldings, and by elaborated rusticated quoins similar to,

but not the same as those at the Boltons. In addition, the traditional linear hall is sometimes modified, with a dog-leg staircase leading out of it at right angles, and a hall floor ceiling height of approximately 13 feet, compared with 12 feet in the smaller houses. The larger houses also sometimes have a handsome curved door to the main reception room. Both types of house have impressive reception rooms, with lavish plaster ceiling decorations, and massive doors well suited to the wide crinolines of the 1860s.

Unfortunately, no original plans have come to light which would show precisely the uses of the rooms in these large family houses. We do not even know whether they originally had bathrooms. Each house would have had one or perhaps two flush toilets, for preoccupation with the pollution of drinking water led to the abolition of cesspits in 1847, and the Public Health Act of the following year made it obligatory for every household to have a fixed sanitary arrangement of some kind. From then on local authorities competed in the laying of sewers and discharge of sewage, at first directly into the Thames, but later, after the "great stink" of the hot summer of 1857, into Sir Joseph Bazalgette's magnificent sewage system. This re-routed the outflow to discharge into the Thames further downstream. So there would certainly have been water closets, but bathrooms were another matter. So long as domestic servants were available, there was little inducement to abandon the age-old, comfortable arrangement of a hip bath or sponge bath before the fire in a dressing room or bedroom. At the time when Tidey was building, hip baths, slop pails, chamber pots and housemaids' sinks were much in use, and it is not until the 1870s that it was customary for bathrooms with fixed plumbing and hot and cold water to be regarded as essential in new houses. This is not to say that Tidey's 1860s houses did not have bathrooms, for plans of some other local buildings do show them, but we do not know.

The larger style of late Tidey houses: grand fenestration and more elaborate stucco detail.

PHOTOGRAPH BY MARY SHENAI

A later-period rear bay window by Tidey with its distinctive curved glass. PHOTOGRAPH BY MARY SHENAI

39 Buckland Crescent, one of Tidey's early houses.

CAMDEN LOCAL STUDIES AND ARCHIVE CENTRE

46 Belsize Square: Tidey's second style, with two windows combined into one.

GLC ARCHITECTURAL DEPARTMENT

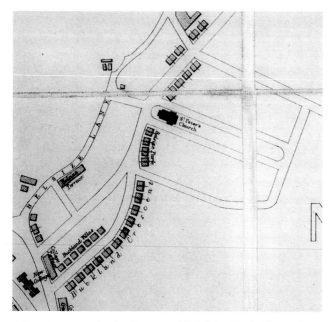

Tideytown in 1862, in Weller's map, showing Tidey's houses in Buckland Crescent and the south side of Belsize Park. In the map on page 69 can be seen the extent of Tidey's further building development. CAMDEN LOCAL STUDIES AND ARCHIVE CENTRE.

Advertisements in the *Ham and High* in 1872 (the earliest year for which copies survive) make almost no mention of bathrooms, though a rare exception offers rooms in Belsize Park Terrace and a bathroom "fitted up with hot and cold water"– evidently an asset to be noted.

Even to the end, Tidey continued to assert his belief that ostentation and large-scale building and tall rooms would attract customers. But there is no doubt that he was beset by worries from the start. He moved from house to house as they were built and awaiting sale (poor Mrs Tidey!) and sought finance wherever he could. An advertisement in *The Builder* in April 1862 states: "Belsize Park Hampstead. Land to be let for building with roads and sewers all complete. For further particulars apply on the Estate at Mr Tidey's office 20 Belsize Park."

He finally worked his way down Belsize Park Gardens, but the houses did not sell quickly enough. It was all to no avail. He evidently overreached himself and, after his bankruptcy in 1870, that was the end of him as a builder.

But not of the Tidey family.

The family, both before and after Daniel the builder, has been extensively researched by two present-day Tidey relatives, Merle Rafferty and Marion Medhurst (both Tideys by birth), to whom I am much indebted for the following abbreviated account.

We first hear of the family living in Washington, Sussex, in the early eighteenth century when John Tydee (as it was then spelt) was a brick-maker. A grandson of his, John Tidey (1773–1849), was an artist, poet and schoolmaster. The family by now show an artistic and talented bent which has continued to this day in Marion Medhurst. John and his wife, Elizabeth, feature in a memoir that Merle Tidey (using her maiden name) wrote in 1983 about her great-great-great-grandfather, containing extracts from their letters and poems. Like so many eighteenth-century literate people, John has a tendency to express his feelings in verse that is prolific rather than memorable. "In no soft vale can we repose from care/Without a thorn to give us anguish there," he writes, in a long poem on the death of their first-born baby son. Other poems and letters to his wife, including an account of a journey on foot, reveal the family set in the eighteenth-century countryside. The memoir also contains reproductions of portraits of this serious, bespectacled couple, presumably painted by their son Alfred, who became a well-known painter and miniaturist, an Academician and a friend and admirer of John Constable.

Our builder, Daniel, was born in 1816 into another branch of the family. Having learnt his trade from his father, a builder in Washington, where the family had

Daniel Tidey the younger and his New Zealand sons, 1910.

MARION MEDHURST

continued to live and prosper, Daniel came to London, hoping no doubt to make his fortune in the widespread opening up of the great estates. By the time he arrived in Belsize, he was married for the second time, and his children were continuing the family's artistic tradition. In the 1871 census we find one of his daughters, Clara, listed as an art student, and later we hear that she contributed a picture to the Society of Lady Artists' exhibition gallery in 1885, which was said to be "Not bad. Audaciously strong in colour and execution." Her name appears in the *Dictionary of Victorian Artists* within the entry for Alfred Tidey, miniaturist and portrait painter.

Of Daniel's other children (there were seven by his first wife and five by his second, after he came to Belsize) we have few details, except that his son Daniel, the eldest son of the second marriage, emigrated to New Zealand in 1883, one year after his father's death, leaving behind a wife and three small children. When Daniel the younger arrived in New Zealand, he put it about that his father was a brilliant mathematician and his uncle a Harley street surgeon. In New Zealand he established himself as a builder of another Tidey Town, and in 1890, after the

appropriate interval for the annulment of marriage when one partner is 'beyond the seas', he married again. A photograph from about 1910 shows Daniel surrounded by four serious New Zealand sons, all with identical noses and highly polished shoes. Only Daniel, in the centre, has a half smile, and a steady gaze which resembles the bright eyes of some of the Tideys today.

After his bankruptcy, Daniel the elder retired to the Belsize Tavern, where he had had the foresight to install one of his daughters as the publican. Between them the Tideys ran both the Washington Hotel in England's Lane and the Belsize Tavern. (He had built both these pubs himself at an early stage of the building operations: a useful arrangement, for pubs served builders and their labourers as a convenient meeting point for hiring to take place and wages to be paid, and spent.) Daniel died at the Belsize Tavern in 1882, and was buried in Hampstead graveyard.

Probate of Daniel's will was not applied for by his second wife, who thereby missed out on £4,000 which he left to her, despite his bankruptcy. This went to a daughter by his first marriage. In addition to this he left "the Master Builder's treasures". Unfortunately these have not been traced, but they are known to be, not the expected trowel and spirit level of his trade, but a cabinet of cherished porcelain pieces.

After his death, the Washington passed into other hands, and in the 1890s received a facelift and redecoration in the style of that decade which remains to this day. It was at this time, presumably, that a crafty association with George Washington was introduced by creating the handsome tiled decoration in the side entrance depicting the great American, and a painted (now repainted) external sign to match. But it is from Washington, Sussex, the birthplace of the Tidey ancestors, that the pub actually derived its name.

Above: The Washington Hotel, built by Tidey.

Left: The Washington Hotel was not named after George Washington; he seems to be laughing at the error.

Right: The Belsize Tavern, which Tidey built, later lived in and finally died in.

PHOTOGRAPHS BY MARY SHENAI

But we are still not at the end of the story, for, in Belsize Park in 1978, two hopeful young men applied at the Washington looking for work. Though their names were Terry and William Tidey, they did not know that it was their great-great-great grandfather who had built that fine pub (now a Grade 2 listed building) back in the 1870s. Terry is now the publican at the Washington, with his wife and family. This marvellous family coincidence was only revealed to him as a result of the researches of Marion Medhurst and Merle Rafferty into their family history.

Despite all his high ambitions, Daniel Tidey could not hold back the flow of changing tastes and fashions. The uniformity of his houses in 1870 (which 100 years later was to cause Camden Council to set up a conservation area) was his downfall. Originality became the new attraction.

William Willett

It is almost as if William Willett was waiting in the wings to take over from Tidey. Having started in business as a stonemason, monumental sculptor and manufacturer of marble chimney pieces, he took over land to the north of Tidey's estate, and started building in Belsize Crescent in 1876, initially living in one of his own houses there. These identical houses are a somewhat cramped version of Tidey's houses. Only the rather quirky dormers, now sadly reduced in number, which are of the tunnel variety and topped with a spherical finial, give any indication of the flamboyance that is to come.

There is a problem about the naming of the architectural styles of houses built in the later part of the

"Originality became the new attraction"; 45 Eton Avenue, one of Harry Measure's earlier houses for the Willetts.

GLC ARCHITECTURAL DEPARTMENT

around the studio house of Sir Frederic Leighton, bore a strong resemblance to Old Holland House, a Jacobean mansion in whose grounds the Holland Park Road studios were built. Certainly the Dutch flourishes that found their way to many of the houses in Eton Avenue and nearby show the same lineage.

At the end of the 1890s, there was a further significant change in style and fashion in suburban house building. It is well represented in the Willett firm's building in the central section of Eton Avenue and in Elsworthy Road and Wadham Gardens houses. By now Willett's son, William Willett the younger, had joined the firm. He had employed a new architect, Ernest Newton, for his own house in Chislehurst, Kent, whose design became the inspiration for the later Willett houses designed by William Faulkner. Now we begin to see a decisive move away from the previous classical styles. The new fashion, then being pioneered in Bedford Park in west London, introduced a more horizontal element. The houses were wider and somewhat lower and, most significantly, the windows ceased to be long-paned sashes, stacked precisely one above another, but were formed by the amalgamation of small-paned casement windows alongside one another in groups, in which the horizontal axis was longer than the vertical (an innovation foreshadowed by Tidey in Buckland Crescent). We are so used to such windows now, since the trend continued well into the twentieth century (in the 1930s even the window panes themselves became horizontal), that we cannot realise how innovative and fashionable such changes must have seemed for these new houses in the suburbs. Even the fanciful houses which were designed by Harry Measures for the Willetts less than a decade earlier, and already built at the outer ends of Eton

nineteenth century. The terms Arts and Crafts, Queen Anne and Aesthetic Movement are used almost interchangeably, and always uncomfortably. But the buildings themselves exhibit one thing in common, that they all attempt to break away from the predominantly classical styles. There is an implied assertion that other styles, not only Gothic, but also French, Dutch, Moorish and even more humble English country styles, may be used as inspiration for building.

Willett's first architect, Harry Measures, in taking advantage of this change of fashion, may well have been influenced by a prestigious group of studio houses recently built in Holland Park Road for artists who were at the pinnacle of fashion. Some of these houses, clustered

The neo-classical porch of 58 Eton Avenue.
GLC ARCHITECTURAL DEPARTMENT

been mirror images of one another, do not bear much resemblance in internal layout.

For the later Willett houses were innovative inside, too. There is a serious attempt to get away from the regular town-house pattern. No longer does the entrance give on to a narrow, straight hall with the stairs opposite. Now a porch and vestibule leads to a squareish hall in the middle of the house, which can be made more room-like by appropriate furnishing, and has the stairs graciously rising from it, usually at right angles to the entrance. More emphasis is also given to the domestic quarters, which, though well segregated, are at ground floor level, and are expanded to include the scullery, pantry, wash-house and a large coal store, as well as the usual kitchen arrangements. By now, of course, a bathroom with fixed plumbing has become essential, and there is a WC on the ground floor as well as the first, and another with access from the back yard.

The Willett houses rightly enjoyed a reputation for good quality and fine finish. All had elegant rooms (even though they were no longer necessarily of classical proportions), with much plaster decoration, alcoves beneath the wide shallow arches which were becoming increasingly popular in Edwardian architecture, and fine timber staircases rising from the hall. In addition, in this quest for the aesthetic, wood panelling and stained and decorated glass were extensively used, with small medallions of painted glass depicting birds and naturalistic scenes set into larger designs of coloured glass, and the whole in marked contrast to the large, clear panes of Tidey's classical Italianate houses. Meticulous detail is even shown in the provision of a metal plumbing chart for each house for the guidance of future users.

Who were these Willetts whose widespread building

Avenue, must have seemed old hat, with their regular vertical windows with small-paned upper sections.

The new-style windows were all part of the attempt to break away from uniformity. The facades of the houses might now portray different historical styles, sometimes merely in the arrangement of the windows, or in the use of red brick, tile-hung fronts, and steeply pitched and gabled roofs, or sometimes in the use of stone mullions and heavy oak doors. These large, detached family houses aim to be unique. Even the two pairs of semi-detached Willett houses at the bottom of Belsize Park Gardens, which might have

High fashion: the arts and crafts façade of 13 Eton Avenue – an impressively bold and rapid change of direction for the Willetts.

GLC ARCHITECTURAL DEPARTMENT

was a coal merchant. We hear of their 15-year-old son, William, as a stone mason's apprentice in 1851. He eventually made his way to London, where his marble fireplaces presumably found favour in Belsize, and he began his meteoric building career.

How the family became involved in Sussex, where they also carried on building operations, and eventually moved into opulent houses in Hove and Chislehurst, is not clear. (There were Willetts in Sussex at the beginning of the nineteenth century, but no relationship has so far been established.)

I am much indebted for what follows to Marjorie Seldon, great-granddaughter of William Willett the elder and great-niece of his son, the daylight-saving William. She remembers visiting their house, an imposing, dark mansion, with servants and a service lift. In her book Poppies and Roses, she writes about her parents, Wilfred and Eileen, and her own childhood in Sussex. Of her great-grandfather, the elder William, she records that he was known to have a violent temper, and "had once thrown a gravy tureen at a maid. In his younger days he liked drinking and smoking and swearing and, as my grand-mother (his daughter-in-law) put it, liked the company of flighty women. All was changed (except his sometimes violent temper) by a vision, the details of which were unclear, but after which he became excessively religious. When my grandmother was newly married, around 1885, she said it was irksome to see letters brought in by the Sunday post and not be allowed to open them until Monday.

"He had a rule book for his workmen which was strongly influenced by his religious principles. A man would be dismissed instantly if discovered drinking or smoking on site. But although strict, he was careful of his

activities in London and the south-east brought prosperity to themselves, and a fashionable breath of change to the new suburb of Belsize Park? Of Huguenot stock, they had arrived in England from France some time after the revocation of the Edict of Nantes in 1685, when Louis XIV finally abandoned all pretence at protection of this well organised Protestant minority. There were, to quote from the *Encyclopaedia Britannica*, two million Huguenots, "the best and thriftiest citizens in the land... and it is said that more than a million escaped from their inhospitable homeland." Over half the manufacturing industry of France was crushed by their departure. But as we know, France's loss was England's gain in many crafts and skills.

The Willetts settled in Colchester, Essex, where in 1845 Everard Willett bequeathed to his dear wife "the use of my household furniture, plate, linen, and china with the coal warehouse, blacksmiths shop, lighters, and stable", for he

A *window at 7 Wadham Gardens, showing the finely wrought detailing of these houses.* GLC ARCHITECTURAL DEPARTMENT

employees' welfare. The men were allowed to work only in daylight hours, averaging 51 [*a week*] in summer and 47 in winter. Safety rules were rigidly enforced: no man must be asked to work in a dangerous position. Everyone had to pay into an Accident and Sickness Fund. He was a good employer, too, to the firm's horses. They could get depressed, he said, if they were left standing in the rain or a strong east wind, and if the roads were muddy their loads should be reduced from 600 to 500 bricks."

Marjorie Seldon also recalls her great-uncle Will, William Willett the younger. He also played a leading role in the building firm, which he officially took over in 1906, following a complicated agreement with a final purchase price of more than a quarter of a million pounds. But his interest was not confined to building. His inventive mind led him elsewhere, and the story goes that, as he rode over Chislehurst Common early on dark winter mornings, he conceived the idea that in winter the clock might be put back by an hour to provide more daylight for industrious early risers. He campaigned for the general introduction of this daylight saving scheme, although it was not adopted until the year after his death in 1915. He also invented the petrol-operated Willett Light Generator, designed to provide electric light for country houses without gas or electricity. The machine, of which there is a detailed account in an article by C. P. Read in *Country Life*, 24th May 1984, could operate up to 15 or 20 lights for ten hours on a gallon of petrol. He also engaged in financial speculation, perhaps to the disadvantage of the building firm. It was also to the detriment of his own health, for, on returning from investigation of his coalmining assets in Spain, he caught a chill and died of pneumonia. The Willett empire continued, but in an altered form, the building interest being separated from the larger estate agency business.

So that is the story of how Tidey and the Willetts brought stucco and brick to cover Belsize, where once, in 1721, in the grounds of the old Belsize House, "The Park, Wilderness and Gardens, being wonderfully Improv'd, and fill'd with variety of Birds which compose a most Melodious and Delightsome Harmony. Every Morning, at Seven a Clock the Music begins to play and continues the whole Day thro'; and Persons inclined to walk and divert themselves in the Morning, may as cheaply breakfast there on Tea and Coffee, as in their own Chambers."

It sounds delightful, but nevertheless, we are grateful to you, Mr Tidey and Mr Willett, for building these fine houses for us and future generations to enjoy.

A footnote: The curved glass that Daniel Tidey used in the rear bay windows of his later houses is known in the trade

Above: William Willett the younger.

*Right: The staircase at
22 Lyndhurst Gardens.*

as bent glass. It seems very likely that these window panes were made for Tidey by Bowden, a firm of glass benders established in Holborn in 1800, although unfortunately there are no surviving records. The firm is now called Bowden-Ide. The method consists of heating a pane of ordinary window glass over a metal mould until it bends on the mould, and allowing it to cool slowly. The process is the same today as it was then, except that gas is used as the fuel instead of coke and wood. The cost of replacing one of the full-length panes today is about £300.

BIBLIOGRAPHY

Merle Tidey, a typed and hand-written script deposited in 1983 in Camden Archive, where it received the title *Daniel Tidey, Builder*.

The Tideys of Washington, Sussex, 1773–1973, Merle Tidey, Dragon, North Wales.

Poppies and Roses, Marjorie Seldon, Sevenoaks E & L, 1985.

"Willett Built", *Victorian Society Journal*, David Prout, 1989.

The Victorian House, John Marshall and Ian Wilcox, OUP, 1986.

Sweetness and Light, Mark Girouard, Sidgwick & Jackson, 1977.

BELSIZE PARK 1870–1914

By 1870, through the efforts of Daniel Tidey and the other developers described by Sir John Summerson and Mary Shenai, Belsize had become 'Belsize Park' and the Chalcots area 'South Hampstead'. An influx of the comfortably-off had conferred upon this area of London (as it had unambiguously become) an identity of a kind, and a repute among the inner suburbs inferior perhaps only to Kensington and St John's wood. But it remained an 'in-between' area, set precariously between the unconstrainable metropolis and the smaller, more select nucleus of Hampstead, which was gathering a southward momentum of its own. At a few points the great city and the venerable suburban village already touched, for instance along the ancient line of Haverstock Hill and Rosslyn Hill, where intermittent ribbon development had sprung up. But there were still great patches of green. Some of these survived right down to the turn of the century, when the Eton and Middlesex Cricket Ground, the final barrier against complete absorption into London, gave way to the handsome Edwardian villas of Elsworthy Road and Wadham Gardens. The story of Belsize Park between 1870 and 1900 is that of the whittling away of one patch after another, normally on large freehold estates where building had already started, and of their replacement with high-class speculative housing of one variety or another.

Before 1870, Belsize Park and the Chalcots estate were more or less defined by their solitude; their houses clustered around the protective, dignifying towers of St Peter's, Belsize Square and St Saviour's, Eton Road, two wholly typical ragstone churches of the 1850s. Since 1900, when almost everything had been built up, the district (like many other suburbs) has been increasingly defined and named by its underground stations: Belsize Park and Chalk Farm on the Northern Line (opened in 1907), and Swiss Cottage (opened on the Metropolitan Line in 1868, transferred to the Bakerloo in 1939–40 and more recently to the Jubilee). However, in estimating the original success of Belsize Park as a residential area, not to be forgotten are the once-flourishing 'overground' stations, all distant enough not to detract from local amenity, yet within walking distance for the vigorous Victorian commuter. Of these, Hampstead Heath and Finchley Road stations on the North London Line opened in 1860, the original Chalk Farm (now Primrose Hill Station) in 1850, and the Midland Railway's Finchley Road station in 1868. This criss-cross of lines, judges Michael Thompson in his history of Hampstead, had small impact on the first development of Belsize Park. In so far as developers were wary of building on top of the several tunnels which ran beneath the area, the railways may even have slowed

A n d r e w   S a i n t

Editor's note: This article appeared in the 1986 edition of this book.

England's Lane in about 1900, looking east towards Haverstock Hill.

CAMDEN LOCAL STUDIES AND ARCHIVE CENTRE

things down. Yet after 1870 all these overland stations were open and working, and they must have greatly aided the 'infilling' process.

A district's public buildings and shops also help to define it. In Belsize Park, the erection in 1878 of the Hampstead Vestry Hall (later Hampstead Town Hall) at the junction of Haverstock Hill and Belsize Avenue confirmed that Hampstead's centre of gravity had shifted southwards, and probably did something to stimulate local shops and enterprises. S S Teulon's noble, purple-brick church of St Stephen's at the top of Pond Street had already in 1869 given notice that Haverstock Hill was not going to

be backward in ecclesiastical assertiveness; while Alfred Waterhouse's Lyndhurst Road Congregational Church, added across the road in 1883, kept up that tradition most ably. But churches and chapels were sadly 'overbuilt' in these years, so that both have gone out of use, and St Stephen's, artistically the most ambitious building in the whole Belsize district, was until recently still awaiting rescue while lesser churches flourished.

As for the shopping itself, the growth of the three centres of Belsize Village, England's Lane and Haverstock Hill around the Belsize Park tube station helped gradually to knit the various separate residential estates together. But until recent years they remained very local in their scope.

Strolling around the streets of Belsize Park and of other comparable London suburbs, one is struck by the length of time which it took for the classical tradition to die in Victorian domestic architecture. Despite their Gothic churches, the stucco dwellings of the Chalcots estate and Belsize Park proper show no greater deviancy from classicism than an innocent, picturesque bargeboard or two. Belsize Park Gardens and its neighbours, indeed, are more boastfully classical than the earlier Chalcots houses.

This goes on well beyond 1870. Thereafter the classical detail is coarsened, but scarcely diminished. The stucco is stripped off the houses by degrees, at first to first-floor level and then down to the ground, while the brickwork revealed is at first grey or off-white, later a richer brown or red. Houses of this kind were being built in the Belsize Avenue and Lambolle Road areas well into the 1880s. After 1890, the tradition of the large, leasehold London house begins to decay as the middle classes are increasingly seduced by flats in the city centre or by more informal freehold houses with bigger gardens in the outlying suburbs. Though Belsize Park holds its own very well in comparison with other inner suburbs at this date, such as Earl's Court, it too is dramatically affected by the collapse of the housing market in the 1890s, and the average house built thereafter is much smaller. The best place to see this is in the small-scale Edwardian streets for clerks built within easy reach of the Belsize Park tube station, Glenloch, Glenmore and Howitt Roads; twenty years before, this land would have been appropriated for much larger houses.

So it was not classicism, but rather the London middle-class house, which died out around 1895. Nevertheless, in the twenty years before this the old classical London house-type was the object of a strong reaction, in which Belsize Park played a prominent part. This reaction is commonly labelled with the confusing but handy title 'Queen Anne'.

This secular aesthetic movement emanated chiefly from metropolitan artists and architects, of whom Belsize Park, by virtue of its nearness to Hampstead, enjoyed more than a fair share.

It grew out of the Gothic Revival. During the 1860s, a tiny handful of architects and artists had played around tentatively with building houses in a Gothic style in London. The most remarkable instance in the area is a battered but still imposing pair of houses at the corner of Lyndhurst Road, Nos. 1-3 Lyndhurst Terrace, built in 1864 for the stained-glass designer Alfred Bell and his brother-in-law John Burlison by a young architect called Charles Buckeridge. Bell took over the whole house after Burlison's death, extended it, and put in some splendid stained glass and mural decorations, some of which survive.

But one-off solutions like Bell's house were too quirky and unsaleable for the speculative builder. The Queen Anne style really developed as a toned-down version of Gothic individualism for the domestic market, with classical details on a Gothic body. The man who introduced it to Belsize Park was Thomas Batterbury, whose father had built the rather weary houses of Parkhill Road and Upper Park Road. Instructively, Batterbury junior specialised in studios and studio houses. The former are simply two sets of single-storey erections tucked away on back land: The Mall Studios, behind the east side of Parkhill Road (1872), and Steele's Studios (1874), off Haverstock Hill between Steele's Road and England's Lane. Another group of this kind, not apparently Batterbury's, is Wychcombe Studios (1879–80), off England's Lane. These show that there was a real local demand for artists' studios.

Architecturally more noteworthy are the two prominent enclaves of studio houses built in the district by Thomas

1-3 Lyndhurst Terrace by Charles Buckeridge.
Toned-down Gothic for a porch in Chalcot Gardens.

PHOTOGRAPHS BY MARY SHENAI

Batterbury and his partner W.F. Huxley. The earlier ones, Nos. 35-39 Steele's Road (1872–5), were spotted long ago by Summerson as 'a most eloquent record of a moment of change in English taste'. All were built for painters, mostly water-colourists, and have (or had) north-facing studios high up at the back looking over the gardens. All are in red brick, out of fashion in London houses for the previous hundred years, and all are blatantly individualistic in plan and eclectic in detail, with entrances sometimes at the sides, big gables in places and prominent roofs. Yet, engagingly, they still have a sniff of the St John's Wood or Chalk Farm villa about them. Batterbury and Huxley's lovely later studio houses in Hampstead Hill Gardens, east of Haverstock Hill (1875–81) show Queen Anne in more refined, sometimes positively Georgian mood. There

is a first hint about them of Norman Shaw, who had just built himself a house in Ellerdale Road up the hill, and whose architecture was to have a great impact upon the later houses of Belsize Park. But they also suggest that the artists for whom Batterbury built had much sympathy and nostalgia for the genuine Georgian architecture of old Hampstead.

After 1880, Queen Anne becomes widespread in Belsize Park, but most of it is as stale as the stucco classical detailing which it replaces. One exponent of merit, however, was Horace Field, a young architect and friend of Shaw, who built some decent flats and houses on the south side of Wedderburn Road from 1884 onwards. Far greater in extent and influence was the work of the Willetts. There were two William Willetts: the father (1837–1913), who

Left: The Gothic influence: the porch of 33 Belsize Avenue.

Above: Gable at 71 Eton Avenue.

GLC ARCHITECTURAL DEPARTMENT

began as a builder by taking over from Daniel Tidey on the Belsize Park estate, and the son (1856–1915), who made the firm's reputation and is known best as 'the inventor of daylight saving'. The Willetts built extensively also in Kensington, Chelsea, Chislehurst and Hove, and after 1880 consistently produced houses of higher comfort and elegance than other speculative builders of their day. At Belsize Park the elder Willett began with Belsize Crescent (1869–75), where the houses are of the dull grey-brick-and-stucco variety. Next followed some big, orthodox 1870s houses along Belsize Avenue.

After a brief gap, the Willetts came back to the district in the early 1880s with a new architect, Harry Measures,

and in two locations (Eton Avenue and Lyndhurst Gardens) started turning out a series of houses which Thompson nicely characterises as 'Norman Shaw on the production line – an endlessly inventive galaxy of gables and bays, chimneys and porches, gryphons and baubles, all built in a medley of ruddy colours. Compared with the Willetts' later productions these houses are coarse, but they have far greater conviction than the average Queen Anne villa. What is more, they enjoyed high standards of fittings and services.

Roy Allen's recent researches on Lyndhurst Gardens show that the Willetts were not immune from the cold wind which blew through the middle-class housing market from 1885 onwards, and the houses proved slow to dispose of; but sell in the end they did. Lyndhurst Gardens itself is not now what it was, but in Eton Avenue and the neighbouring Strathray Gardens one can still feel the force

Above: "...gryphons and baubles":
detail of 57 Eton Avenue.

Right: 38 Eton Avenue.

GLC ARCHITECTURAL DEPARTMENT

*Left: Conservatory window,
57 Eton Avenue.*

*Above: Door furniture in
21 Elsworthy Road.*

GLC ARCHITECTURAL DEPARTMENT

Robert Bevan's studio in Adamson Road.

PHOTOGRAPH BY MARY SHENAI

of Measures' verve and the Willetts' drive. Later again they brought in a quieter architect, Amos Faulkner. He designed most of the longer, lower houses built at the east end of Eton Avenue and, more numerously, in Elsworthy Road and Wadham Gardens, the Willetts' final 'take' in the district. Put up between 1895 and 1903, they buck the trend of the time towards smaller houses or flats. They adopt a more suburban 'Old English' style, again largely derived from Norman Shaw via his pupil Ernest Newton, who had worked with the Willetts at Chislehurst. These

richly detailed houses are every bit as good as anything built at Hampstead Garden Suburb, which they actually antedate by a few years.

After 1900, additions to the Belsize Park area amounted mainly to smaller infilling or replacement. One or two special buildings of the Arts and Crafts years are worth singling out. The Belsize Fire Station at the corner of Lancaster Grove (1914–15), with its fine brick tower, is commonly held to be the masterpiece of CC Winmill, perhaps the ablest of the many interesting architects who

Voysey's addition to the artist Arthur Rackham's house at 16 Chalcot Gardens. GLC ARCHITECTURAL DEPARTMENT

by aesthetes sauntering around its well-tree'd streets. In 1881, for instance, Belsize Park (the street) seems to have been inhabited almost exclusively by prosperous tradesmen, merchants, professionals and their dependants. At No. 16 there is one obscure architect, at No. 69 one female author. The most interesting residents are John Jackson at No. 3, papier-mâché manufacturer, employing 275 men and 16 boys; at No. 34 Coleman Defries, gas engineer and chandelier maker; and at No. 60, Daniel Howard, employing 60 hands in the cabinet-making firm of Howard and Sons. At No. 25 lives the proprietor of a lunatic asylum (not on the premises), at No. 26 a chicory, cocoa and mustard manufacturer and merchant. Belsize Park is a street of above-average prosperity, but the mixture is not untypical.

The lesser houses of Belsize Crescent make a poorer professional showing at the same date, with the occasional inhabitant clearly letting out rooms and starting the street on the slippery slope of multi-occupation. In compensation, there are three clergymen. Most houses here have two or three servants; one or two have only one, and an American merchant boasts four. This pattern of two or three servants per house is repeated all over Belsize Park, even in the artistic ghettos of Steele's Road and Hampstead Hill Gardens. Who lived in the Willett houses of Eton Avenue and Elsworthy Road we shall not know in detail until the 1891 census becomes available[1], but a similar tone is suggested by the directories.

worked for the early London County Council. There is also a quiet little brick addition by C F A Voysey at No. 16 Chalcot Gardens (1898). This again was done for an artist, and on inspection it will be found that the whole rectangle between England's Lane and Steele's Road appears to have been an artistic preserve. Even the hefty houses of Chalcot Gardens reveal studios high up along their fronts. Some other pleasant houses of the later 'Willett type', probably of about 1900, are to be seen along Lawn Road.

Finally, what do the censuses and directories tell us about the denizens of Belsize Park in these years? Certainly they caution us against imagining the district as peopled

1. *The 1891 census was published in 1992, after this article was written.*

*Every bit as good as anything built at Hampstead Garden
Suburb ; 15 Eton Avenue, an important house tragically
demolished in 1993; its replacement is shown on page 109.*

GLC ARCHITECTURAL DEPARTMENT

THE AMERICAN CIVIL WAR COMES TO BELSIZE PARK

"North London has had its share of controversial vicars", said the *Ham and High* in 1997. "But it appears that no modern man of the cloth can compare with the Rev. Francis W Tremlett, Vicar of Belsize Park from 1860 to 1913."

Frank Tremlett's father, Robert, was born in 1797. He studied medicine at Barts in 1814–15, and became an army surgeon in Newfoundland, where he died in 1842. His mother, Elizabeth Way Dare, was born at Exeter in 1801. Frank was born in Newfoundland in 1821. At 14 he went to school at Quincy, near Boston, and at 17 to Governor Dummer Academy in Massachusetts. In 1842 he returned to Newfoundland, studied theology at St John's and became a priest in 1846.

From then until 1849 he served the fishing communities at Portugal Cove near St John's. His diaries for this period show that his first concern was for his parishioners' souls, and he demanded full formal religious observance from them. Behind this was a concern for the spiritual and social benefits that would flow from an ordered society, which explains much in his later life, including his passionate involvement in the American Civil War.

In January 1849, he took ship for England, and his diary relates in graphic detail what a voyage it was, with the ship coming close to sinking and the passengers recruited to help empty the hold to lighten ship.

Once ashore, he seems to have been in a hurry to get to London to see a Mrs Josephine Dare, née Scarlett, the widow of a relative of Frank's mother. Without warning, on 22nd February 1849, his diary notes: "Thursday. Sealed my fate. Went to St Johns Church & was married. Drove to the Railway Station & found myself... in Southampton."

Josephine was well connected – a niece of the first Lord Abinger, and first cousin once removed of William Scarlett, the third Lord, who was to serve on the staff of his uncle, Sir James Scarlett, at the charge of the Heavy Brigade at Balaklava in 1854. William was then to be Colonel of the Scots Fusilier Guards in Canada during the *Trent* crisis of 1861–2. While there, he married a Helen Magruder; interestingly, her uncle, John Magruder, had recently gone south to become a general in the army of the Confederate States of America.

The diary makes almost no other mention of his wife, but among the addresses in it is 'Miss Scarlett, Erlswood, Surrey'. Earlswood is not far from Abinger Hall, Dorking, the family seat of Lord Abinger; it was also the location of

Michael Hammerson

A watercolour of St Peter's, presented to Tremlett on his jubilee as vicar in 1910.

COURTESY OF J C AND T T FELL

himself; how he could afford it is not clear. It had 1,100 seats, but such was Tremlett's personality and preaching that there was a long waiting list.

Immediately he plunged again into controversy. Writing to the Bishop of London about the church's name, he observed, "It has been spoken of as St Peter's, but... I should... prefer to make it a memorial of some great proof of our Lord's Divinity. In the Protestant Episcopal Church of America, Churches are... called the Church of the Ascension.., the Nativity.., the Crucifixion, &c... I would prefer to make the [stained glass windows] represent these facts of Our Lord's life, to that of the History of St Peter, however good an apostle he might have been"!

There was also an acrimonious exchange over new galleries. The Bishop thought Tremlett was trying to get a free pew, and Tremlett and his churchwardens exploded. They wrote: "My Lord... we feel bound to say that if the decision... is final your Lordship will have deprived this Parish, in the opinion of... every Parishioner, without a single exception, of a great and lasting benefit. There is no other way of providing accommodation for the number of residents whom we are... obliged to send away.

"Your Lordship has not understood the proposed assignment of one of the pews to the Tremlett house. It is not intended to assign to the *incumbent*, but to the founder of the Church. Mr Tremlett built the Church at his own private cost... [and never] stipulated for a pew... As regards the pecuniary question to which your Lordship alludes... Mr Tremlett... is happily placed beyond the reach of all considerations of this sort..."

To the bishop's stipulation that pews should be set aside for the poor of the parish, they replied "There are no poor

the Royal Earlswood Hospital for the Insane, and, as will be seen later, this may not be coincidental.

By 1853, Tremlett was back in Boston with his new wife and his mother. There, as vicar of St Botolph's, he displayed what was to be a characteristic impatience with authority, defying his bishop by establishing a second church in the poorer part of the city. When he was duly fired, he responded with a furious pamphlet attacking the bishop. He then returned to England, and was vicar of St Andrew's, Enfield, until 1857.

St Peter's, Belsize Park

In 1859, he was living at Foley Place, Well Walk, at the same time as St Peter's Church in Belsize Square was being built to serve the new suburb of Belsize Park. Tremlett was to be its first vicar, and is referred to as its founder. Much of the £9,000 that it cost to build was met by Tremlett

in this parish". A weary bishop filed the letter under the heading 'Mr Tremlett's Galleries'.

That same year, Tremlett gained a doctorate from the University of Jena, Germany; his thesis was a thinly veiled attack on evolutionary theory.

Tremlett moved to 11 Buckland Crescent, and remained there until the new parsonage was built behind the church, also at his expense, in 1862.

The American Civil War

In 1861, America was torn apart by the Civil War. Much hinged on whether Europe would recognise the South. The war generated great debate in England, *The Times* of 20th August 1864 observing that "The country between the Rappahannock and the Potomac has become as familiar [to] the English public as the space between St Paul's and South Kensington". Though he was educated in anti-slavery Boston, Tremlett was for the South. A memorial sketch of 1915 says: "It is to his strong sympathy with the underdog that may be attributed his sympathy for the South. He thought, rightly or wrongly, that the South was coerced by the North, and he did not hesitate for a moment to espouse [its] cause... His house soon became, unofficially... the headquarters of the Confederacy in London..." Another source calls him "among the more prominent and effective of the English propagandists".

Tremlett made the Parsonage a rendezvous for Confederates in England, to the extent that it was locally nicknamed 'Rebel's Roost'. Notable among its visitors was Matthew Fontaine Maury, world-famous for having revolutionised navigation. He resigned from the US Navy at the start of the war, and came to England to purchase arms for the South and aid her diplomatic effort. He and Tremlett became close friends.

Tremlett's album is filled with photographs of Confederate diplomats and naval officers, and surviv-

A photograph of Tremlett with Matthew Fontaine Maury on the latter's receiving an honorary doctorate from Cambridge in 1866.

COURTESY OF
JC AND TT FELL

ing letters attest to their high regard for him. Robert Pegram, commander of the *Nashville*, the first Confederate privateer, wrote to Tremlett's sister Louisa: "I can never repay the obligation I am under to yourself & your dear noble brother for the many acts of generosity & kindness that I have received from you." Charles Morehead, ex-governor of Kentucky, wrote to Confederate President Jefferson Davis in 1864: "The Rev. Tremlett is indefatigable in our behalf and deserves the thanks of every true lover of our country". In 1870 Maury dubbed Tremlett "the best Confederate in England".

The sermon

In 1863, Tremlett gave a pro-Southern sermon, in which he spoke of the Southerners as "a people who have cultivated the affections – nay, have inspired – a servile race, which we originally planted on their shores, with a love and affection for their masters, which have astounded the whole world. They have Christianised that race... There is scarcely a bondsman among the millions there, who might not be free tomorrow if he chose to seek the protection of the invading armies – many have gone, like Onesimus the friend of Paul, back to their masters...

"Let each of the 20,000 parishes of England send up to our rulers a request, as the expression of their Christian feeling, that this demon of war should sheathe his fiery sword..."

Powerful stuff – but based on a romantic illusion, harboured by many Englishmen, of a South where slave and master lived in harmony, and where the Christianised slave was better off than his 'savage' brother in Africa.

Maury thought he could use the sermon to manipulate British opinion, and persuaded Tremlett to publish it. Ten thousand copies were printed, and sent to every church in the land, together with a petition organised under the banner of 'The Society for Obtaining a Cessation of Hostilities in America'. Tremlett was the Society's secretary. The chairman was Admiral Talavera Vernon Anson of 7 College Crescent. Another officer was John Fernyhough of 18 Belsize Park, one of Tremlett's churchwardens (his 25-year-old son was a cotton broker – another possible link to the South). The treasurer, Crewe Aiston, was another churchwarden.

Yet another was Commander Bedford Pim, RN, of Lower Mount Cottage. He had sailed in search of the Arctic explorer Sir John Franklin; been wounded in the China wars in 1858; tried to build a railway across Nicaragua; later became a barrister and MP; and wrote a book, *The Negro & Jamaica* (1866), which was a white supremacist diatribe. Pim helped Tremlett by gaining access to British naval shipyards for Confederate officers.

The petition

Maury persuaded a pro-Southern MP, William Lindsay, to move a resolution in Parliament in July 1864, when Tremlett's petition was to be presented, urging the government to join other European powers in mediating an end to the war. On 15th July 1864, the Marquis of Clanricarde introduced Tremlett's delegation to Prime Minister Palmerston. Tremlett told him that the 13,000-signature petition proved public support for British intercession. But it was far too late, and Palmerston knew it. The Southern defeat at Gettysburg had already ended any chance of foreign recognition; Lincoln's emancipation proclamation had transformed the war, in European eyes, into a war to free the slaves; and the war was now going against the South. Moreover, Palmerston had just survived a political crisis, and no longer needed the support of pro-Southern MPs.

Tremlett and his colleagues continued their efforts, but it was hopeless, and nine months later the Confederacy fell.

The Alabama

Raphael Semmes was Captain of the Confederate warship *Alabama*, which terrorised Northern merchant shipping, sinking over 60 ships during her two-year cruise. Semmes' *Memoirs* tell how he met Tremlett in 1862, while waiting to return to America after the loss of his first ship, the *Sumter*.

"One day whilst I was sitting quietly, after breakfast, in my rooms at Euston Square, running over the column of American news in the 'Times', Commander North entered, and in company with him came a somewhat portly gentleman, with an unmistakable English face, and dressed in clerical garb – not over clerical, either, for, but for his white cravat, and the cut of the collar of his coat, you would not have taken him for a clergyman at all. Upon being presented, this gentleman said to me, pleasantly, 'I have come to take the Captain of the *Sumter* prisoner, and carry him off to my house, to spend a few days with me.' I looked into the genial face of the speaker, and surrendered myself to him a captive at once. There was no mistaking the old time English gentleman – though the gentleman himself was not past middle age – in the open countenance, and kindly expression of my new friend. Making some remarks to him about quiet, he said, 'That is the very thing I propose to give you; you shall come to my house, stay as long as you please, and see nobody at all unless you please'. I dined with him, the next day, .. .and spent several days at his house... It became, in fact, my English home, and was but little less dear to me than my own home in America. The name of the Rev. Francis W. Tremlett, of the 'Parsonage, in Belsize Park, near Hampstead, London,' dwells in my memory, and in that of every other Confederate who ever came in contact with him – and they are not few – like a household word."

In August 1862, despite Northern pressure to impound her, the *Alabama* slipped out of her Liverpool dock, disguised as a merchant ship. After her sinking in 1864, Semmes issued a certificate of service to the survivors, including one to Tremlett, calling him the *Alabama*'s chaplain, although he certainly never sailed on her; perhaps it was a gesture of friendship.

In July 1864 the *Alabama*, in need of repairs, was trapped at Cherbourg by a northern warship. On the 17th, Semmes wrote to Tremlett of his intention to fight; two days later, his ship steamed out to meet the USS *Kearsarge* and a watery grave in the Channel; Semmes was rescued by an English yacht. A few days later, the Confederate agent in Paris, George Sinclair, though busy looking after the sur-

A photograph of Raphael Semmes taken in July 1864, a few days after the loss of his ship, the Alabama.

vivors, wrote Tremlett a long letter to keep him informed.

Soon after the *Alabama*'s sinking, a letter advised *Daily Telegraph* readers, "It has been determined to present Captain Semmes with a handsome sword, to replace that which he buried with his ship. Gentlemen wishing to participate in this testimony to unflinching patriotism, and naval daring, will be good enough to communicate with the chairman, Admiral Anson... or... Bedford Pim".

"Upon my landing in Southampton," Semmes recalled, "I was received with great kindness by the English people... Mr Mason... and the Rev. F. W. Tremlett came post-haste to Southampton.... The latter gentleman... now came to insist that I should go again to my 'English home'... As soon as I had wound up the affairs of the *Alabama*, I went up to enjoy the hospitality of my friend Tremlett, at Belsize Park...

wife in 1877. But they never mention Mrs Tremlett – his first wife Josephine who, we are told, became an invalid, for whom he cared for 23 years, but whom his parishioners never saw. Why was he associating openly, for nearly 20 years, with the woman who was to become his second wife, when his first wife was still alive? Part of the answer lies in the discovery of Josephine's certificate of death in January 1876, aged 66, in the Brooke House Private Lunatic Asylum, Upper Clapton.

The fast boats built to bring arms and supplies to the South through the northern blockade were called blockade runners. Apart from Tremlett's sister Louisa Ann, he had two others in America, Fanny and Isabella. In January 1865, a blockade runner was launched in London called the *Louisa Ann Fanny*; was Tremlett held in such esteem by Southerners that they named it after two of his sisters?

Tremlett had family in Boston. Massachusetts records reveal Henry M Tremlett, Lt.-Col. of the 39th Massachusetts Infantry, a Northern regiment, and a cousin of Frank's, mortally wounded nine days before the end of the war. Much as Frank hated the Yankees, his album contains a picture of Henry, in uniform, suggesting he felt some affection for him, and perhaps even remorse for his death.

The ex-Confederates

Like many Southern sympathisers, Tremlett remained 'unreconstructed'. In an effort to find Raphael Semmes work, he even wrote to Count Bismarck in 1866, recommending Semmes as commander of the Prussian Navy! When the former Confederate President Davis visited England in 1868, his wife Varina wrote to Louisa: "It will afford us great pleasure to dine with you today,

"Here we arranged for a visit.., to the continent... One other gentleman, an amiable and accomplished sister of my friend Tremlett, and two other ladies... accompanied us.... I must... say of my friend Tremlett, that I found him a veteran traveller, who knew how to smooth all the difficulties of a journey..."

Some mysteries

Many Confederates asked to be remembered to a 'Miss Marmont'; Charlotte Marmont became Tremlett's second

Charlotte Marmont, Tremlett's second wife, in the vicarage garden. This photograph also shows the massive vicarage which Tremlett built with his own money in about 1880; it was demolished in 1913.

COURTESY OF JC AND
TT FELL

and then I hope Mr Tremlett and Mr Davis will have out a small part of the long talk which I am sure they will never willingly finish 'till death does them part'".

Semmes temporarily left his sword and a presentation flag with the Tremletts, who displayed them proudly at the Parsonage. Semmes' letters to the Tremletts combined affection for Louisa with bitter tirades against the hated Yankees. "I fear he is still unreconstructed", Louisa wrote in 1867.

After an interlude with the ill-fated Emperor Maximilian of Mexico in 1866, the Maurys lived at 3 Belsize Square. In 1868, when Cambridge awarded Maury an honorary doctorate, Tremlett and Pim organised a testimonial dinner for him, to which the scientific, military and political world came, and Maury was presented with 3,000 guineas. In the same year the Maurys returned to America, to the Tremletts' great sadness.

Other ex-Confederates visited and left their photos – Beauregard, whose special misfortune had been to win the first battle of the war too easily, lulling the Confederates into under-estimating their enemy; Robert E Lee's chief of Staff, the Rev. William Pendleton, who led a vicious post-war campaign to lay blame for Confederate defeat on one of Lee's generals; Lee's chief engineer, Walter Stevens; and, in 1874, one of Lee's daughters, who perhaps gave Tremlett the picture of her father in his album.

The 1867 Lambeth Conference was attended by bishops from all over the world, including the American South, so it was natural that Tremlett should be their Commissioner; and when Bishop Quintard of Tennessee, who had been a Confederate chaplain in the war, sought funds for the University of the South in Tennessee, which had been destroyed during the war, Tremlett set about raising £2,500, saving the University and earning him its first honorary degree. A student's hall was named after him; its site is still called Tremlett Place.

Later years

Tremlett and Charlotte Marmont were married in 1877 by Charlotte's nephew Edgar Sheppard, Canon of Gloucester Cathedral. But why was the Sheppard family – Edgar, and his son Dick, later famous as the 'Radio Vicar' – friendly with the Tremletts? Edgar's father, also Edgar, was Professor of Psychiatry at King's College and head of the Male Wing of the Colney Hatch Asylum. In the 1850s he was in practice at Enfield, when Tremlett was vicar. Perhaps Tremlett met him there and sought his help for Josephine, with the result that they became friends and Tremlett met Charlotte.

Tremlett always remained passionate and combative. In 1876, he published a sermon on "Vivisection: The Duty of Christians with Reference to its Cruelty". Bishop Quintard's diary gives a splendid vignette: "December 31, 1875: The subject of vivisection is just now very much before the public... Tremlett is a rabid anti-vivisectionist and it is something grand to see him warm up. He invariably reaches white heat and does his cause harm by denunciation of all who hold the opposite views..."

Tremlett loved the sea, and bought a yacht, the 78' *Don Roderick*. He would invite anyone he thought would enjoy a day on the sea – East End clergy, parishioners, schools, even local police.

The Rev FW Tremlett in the vicarage conservatory in about 1900.

COURTESY OF
JC AND TT FELL

He also founded a free hostel in Belsize Square for young businessmen who wished to enter the ministry "and devote their lives to combat the alarming increase of Socialism, Atheism, and general depravity in... our great cities", and also the Hampstead Working Men's Institute.

Charlotte died in 1896. In 1901, Louisa wrote that Frank was troubled with "increasing deafness", though "otherwise well and cheerful", but her own death in 1912 was a heavy blow.

In 1910, Tremlett's parishioners presented him with a beautiful illuminated address to celebrate 50 years as their vicar.

On 1st June 1913, in failing health, the 92-year-old Tremlett preached in church for the last time; ten days later he died. We're told that "his death found him in

Tremlett's memorial slab.

PHOTOGRAPH BY M HAMMERSON

need... Like the rock-bound rugged coasts of New-foundland... he was a hardy man. Softness or smoothness of speech or action had no place with him when opposed by what he felt to be wrong... I remember... when I was a boy... that he preached against a false sentimentality which he thought had caught public opinion in reference to some wrong-doers, and it was the same side of his nature which made him undertake his work against Socialism...

"Belsize will seem strange without the neat, old-fashioned familiar figure; we shall miss the cheery 'well, friends', of his greeting. We shall miss the brightness and laughter that he brought with him – he believed in the tonic of laughter rather than of tears. "

A new parsonage was built in 1915 as a memorial to him, and a beautiful memorial slab by Irish sculptress Kathleen Shaw was placed on the south wall of the chancel.

Tailpiece

Tremlett's death only deepened the mystery of his story. Most Confederate records were lost at the end of the war. Tremlett's archives would have proved invaluable, but his memorial sketch of 1915 says: "It is to be regretted that the immense piles of letters received by Dr Tremlett on [the Confederacy] from men of note had all to be destroyed, according to his wish and directions."

the midst of an energetic campaign against socialism". A large funeral procession followed him to Fortune Green cemetery.

At his death he was still working 18 hours a day; the memorial sketch called him "the most wonderful old man in London". The Sunday after his funeral, his congregation was given a sketch of his life in a sermon:

"...the traveller, the philosopher, the yachtsman, the missionary, the scientific man, the enemy to all that savoured of unfairness and which held that might was right, and the tender-hearted to the call of sorrow and

BIBLIOGRAPHY

Tremlett Memorial Fund: With Short Sketch of the Life of the Rev. Francis William Tremlett, DD, DCL, First Vicar (1850–1913) of St Peter's, Belsize Park. Hampstead, NW (c.1915)

A Short History of St Peter's, Belsize Park, Howard Isenberg, c.1970

Memoirs of Service Afloat During the War Between the States, Raphael Semmes, Baltimore, 1869; Greenwich, Conn., 1962; Secaucus, NJ, 1987; Baton Rouge, 1996

ST PETER'S, BELSIZE SQUARE

It is interesting to note that St Peter's is on the site of Belsize House, where, around 1700, an unusual attraction was the institution of 'short marriages' (see Roy Allen's article above) – an institution stopped by law in 1716.

St Peter's Church was consecrated on 11th November 1859. Built on land given by the Dean and Chapter of Westminster, and named after the Abbey (St Peter's, Westminster), it was one of a dozen new churches to be built in Hampstead over a period of only twenty-five years. The benefactors included the first vicar, Dr Francis William Tremlett, who himself paid for the nave, aisle and transepts, while his parishioners took care of the chancel. The church was built at a cost of £9,000, and had seating accommodation for 1,100. The architect was J R St Aubyn Mumford.

The site was conveyed to the Ecclesiastical Commissioners in October 1859, and the surrounding square in 1869.

The ecclesiastical parish was established in 1861, and in the following year Dr Tremlett moved into the new vicarage (see the photograph on page 64). This occupied the lower end of the square, which was called St Peter's Road (North and South) until 1866. At this time there were only about 300 families in the parish.

The church was enlarged in 1875, again by J R St Aubyn

St Peter's, Belsize Square.   KEITH WYNN PHOTOCRAFT

Howard Isenberg

A brief extract, taken by kind permission of the author, from his excellent booklet A Short History of St Peter's Belsize Park

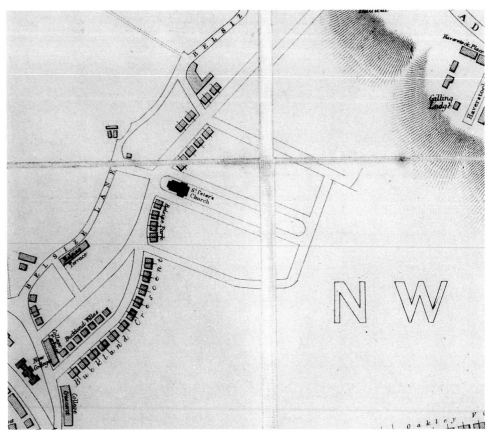

This detail from Weller's map of 1862 shows the newly built St Peter's in what was then St Peter's Square, in the middle of Daniel Tidey's far from complete housing development.

CAMDEN LOCAL STUDIES AND ARCHIVE CENTRE

Mumford, the cost of £2,500 being met mainly by the congregation.

In 1913, the original vicarage, having been declared by the Ecclesiastical Commissioners to be in a poor state, was demolished. A new vicarage was built in 1915, occupying the site of 27–30 Belsize Square. The site of the garden would be thrown into the site of the new house, and part of this was later used for a tennis court.

As the result of a disturbing architect's report of late 1915, an extensive restoration was undertaken, principally to the fabric of the church, and completed in 1917. Exten-sive underpinning was necessary, as the foundations had not been sunk deep enough, nor with due regard to the variation of the virgin soil between the north and south sides of the Church. Evidence of this can be seen to this day. Other costly work included extensive roof repairs, the restoration of crumbling facings, a complete new system of drainage, rebuilding the west window in Portland stone, a new engine for the organ, and rebuilding the vestry and the organ chamber – all this in War years. The whole cost was £4,000. The Church raised £1,500 in a loan from Queen Anne's Bounty and took a bank overdraft, under the

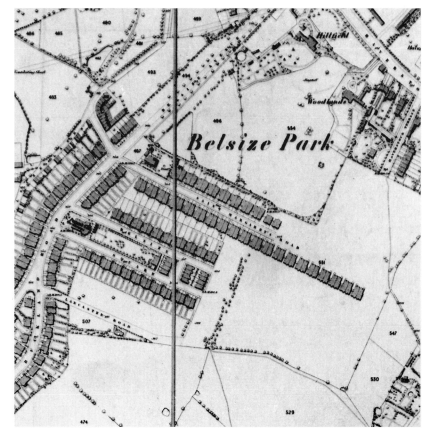

Above: A stained glass window in St Peter's.

PHOTOGRAPH BY JAKE BROWN

Left: By 1872, the vicarage has been built and the ornamental garden laid out.

CAMDEN LOCAL STUDIES AND ARCHIVE CENTRE

churchwardens' personal guarantee of £700, whilst the builders, Messrs Dovey, consented to accept payment of the £900 balance of their account in yearly payments of £100 and interest at 6% over nine years.

In 1927 there were many repairs and alterations. These included the removal of the two original galleries, over the north and south sides of the east transept, and the consequent opening of the organ loft; the silvering of the organ pipes; the raising of the choir stalls, with the addition of one row; removing one pew to make way for steps to the chapel; lowering and moving the pulpit; internal repairs to the organ; and a new boiler. A pamphlet of the time notes that the church had not been redecorated since 1890.

The organ is a Bevington, built in 1841 in another church (unknown) and rebuilt in St Peter's in 1917. It was always sharp in relation to concert pitch, and, although it was tuned down as far as the pipes would allow in 1963, it is still a quarter-tone sharp. The action is pneumatic, with an electric blower that was installed in 1928.

The present vicarage was built in 1953. The old vicarage is now occupied by the Jewish Synagogue, whose evolution is briefly described in the next article.

THE BELSIZE SQUARE SYNAGOGUE

The Belsize Square Synagogue is built around the old vicarage of St Peter's Church, on land which originally was a marshland surrounding the Tyburn Stream, and was part of Belsize Manor.

The three original buildings in the square were the Church, a public house (pulled down in around 1890) and the first vicarage. Built in 1862, this was demolished in 1913 because of its poor structural condition – possibly connected with its location directly over the Tyburn Stream.

The second vicarage was built in 1915–16 on the site of the public house. The architect was Mr Paine, and the building cost £2,500: it had two large reception rooms, a dining room, study, seven bedrooms and a large garden, later sold to a tennis club. This building is now the core of the Synagogue buildings.

During World War Two, the vicarage was used for various clubs, and building alterations included a canteen on the ground floor. The south end of the building was damaged by bombing, and was reconstructed soon after the end of the war.

In the late 1940s, the Church Commissioners became concerned about the size and unsuitability of the vicarage for what was then rather a run–down neighbourhood with a large transient population. A new third vicarage was built, adjoining St Peter's Church, and the old vicarage was sold for £15,000 to Belsize Square Synagogue, originally called the New Liberal Jewish Congregation, in 1947.

For its first years, the congregation had been itinerant, until it settled first in Buckland Crescent and then managed to purchase the war-damaged Old Vicarage in Belsize Square. The founders of the Belsize Square Synagogue came from mainly German-speaking countries, as the neighbourhood attracted many European refugees in the years before, during and after the war.

The vicarage was adapted for the Synagogue community by the architects De Metz and Birks in early 1952, with seating for a hundred congregants – major services were held in local cinemas – plus classrooms, offices and a clubroom.

The increasing prosperity and stability of the Synagogue community enabled the construction of a new Synagogue in 1957/58. The architect was H Walter Reifenberg, who had trained in Germany, at the Bauhaus-inspired Berlin Architecture School, and he designed a building with a deliberately stark interior. However, the exposed internal brickwork was not to everyone's taste, and in 1962 it was covered with hardwood boarding. The Synagogue incorporated a very simple, quiet and effective natural draught ventilation system, which enabled services to be held with all windows closed and with a steady flow of fresh air. In 1973, a simple and economical new

Michael Brod

Above: The present Synagogue.

Right: The gates put up in 1988 and, behind them, the second vicarage, converted into a Synagogue in 1952.

PHOTOGRAPHS BY MARY SHENAI

community hall, designed by Joseph Mendleson, was built on the site of the tennis courts. In 1985 the architects Brod Salmon Partnership began a programme of refurbishing and altering the Belsize Square buildings.

The Belsize Square Synagogue is perhaps somewhat unusual among modern British congregations in its programme of commissioning works of art. This must owe something to the European cultural origins of the synagogue's founders, with their great emphasis on creativity, scholarship, literature and music, and with a blend of traditional and modern values. The collection now includes many of the ritual furnishings of the Synagogue and Hall, and a Holocaust Memorial at Willesden cemetery – the first monument of its type in the country.

The Synagogue's art and architecture are not flamboyant or elaborate. The German phrase 'Neue Sachlichkeit' – often translated as 'new practicality or realism'

– sums up the building's clean, understated, functional style. The works of art, too, are not major masterpieces, but in their own way they are significant and evocative, and a reflection of the community that has quietly evolved in Belsize Square for the past sixty years.

In 1988, decorative metalwork gates were added to the synagogue's main entrance. Their 'Star of David' symbols were the first significant external indication that the buildings are a synagogue, displaying that the community finally felt safe in its local environment.

71

A NEST OF GENTLE ARTISTS

Extracts from
'The history of the Mall Studios in Belsize Park'

Between St Dominic's Priory and the Victorian villas of Parkhill Road, a small pathway leads to the Mall Studios. At first glance this row of seven studios, with one detached studio at the end, gives the impression of small stable-like cottages. Once inside, however, people are immediately struck by their size and height and by the colourful gardens at the back.

The studios were built in 1872 by Thomas Batterbury, to be leased to working artists. Thomas Batterbury was described in a contemporary journal as an avant garde architect. In *The Architect* of 7th August 1872 (reprinted on p 76), there is a detailed description of the building of the Mall Studios, and the interesting thing about it is that many of the features mentioned still remain. The walls of red bricks from Messrs Culverhouse of Hampstead still show on two of the studios, although the others have been painted white. Of the ceilings of open timber construction, 'varnished but not stained', one is still visible in No.1, showing the storage balcony, which in other studios has been converted into an extra bedroom. Originally all the studios had three skylights, one facing east and two facing west. Some of those facing west have been replaced by dormer windows. The small windows facing west were

The Mall Studios today.

Gwen Barnard

Editor's note: This article appeared in the 1986 edition of this book.

Sir George Clausen's famous painting of Haverstock Hill in about 1894 (St Stephen's can be glimpsed at top right).
COURTESY OF BURY ART GALLERY

glazed with 'old-fashioned crown bulls' eyes'. Most of these still exist, though no studio has a full set.

One of the unique features of the studios was that each one had a chimney pot 'specially designed with incised ornaments and bearing the monogram of the owner'. Two of these remain, between No.3 and No.4, the one over No.3 still distinctly showing the monogram of the original resident, William Bright Morris. The Mall Studios are among the very few Victorian studios where so many of the original architectural features are still visible. The roofs are covered with 'red tiles from Messrs Seeley of Bridgewater' and, as the studios are 'conserved', anyone who wishes to renew them has to use the same pattern of tile.

A distinguished occupant of No.4 was George Clausen, later RA, who was there for a period around 1879. Several of his pictures have been purchased by the Tate Gallery. Of the later inhabitants of the studios, a pattern emerges of long-staying serious painters, a tight community in this quiet backwater where no traffic is heard.

One long-staying artist was Cecil Stephenson, who came to No.6 in 1919 and lived there until his death in

1965. According to his note-book he took over the studio from Walter Sickert, but there is no record of Sickert ever having lived there. Stephenson studied at Leeds School of Art, the Royal College of Art and the Slade. He painted in a naturalistic style until 1932, when he produced his first abstract work. He made a mural for the Festival of Britain in 1951 and one of his pictures was bought by the Tate.

Hepworth, Nicholson, Read

In the late 1920s and right up to 1939, the Mall became known as a meeting ground for artists of international reputation. In 1927 two sculptors, Barbara Hepworth and her husband John Skeaping, came to No.7 with their son Paul. In 1931 Ben Nicholson moved to the Mall, married Barbara Hepworth and lived with her in No.7 until 1939. Their children, the Nicholson triplets, lived in another studio from 1934 to 1939. Ben Nicholson has said that his stay in the Mall was one of the happiest periods of his life, and that no one who had not lived there could have any idea of the excitement of the new ideas which resulted from that period.

Herbert Read, the art critic, came to No.3 in 1934. He lived there until 1938 and he, too, described his stay as the happiest time in his life. Read built a hut in the garden of No.3, which is still there, and in which he wrote his one novel, *The Green Child*. He described the atmosphere in the Mall at that period as 'a nest of gentle artists' (thinking of Turgenev's nest of gentle-folk), who met daily to discuss their work. They also planned a number of publications in which they presented their ideas to the general public. These were *Unit One*, edited by Herbert Read; *Circle* (1937), an international survey of

Barbara Hepworth in her studio in about 1932, photographed by Ben Nicholson, whom she had married the previous year.

THE TATE GALLERY ARCHIVE

ist, lived in nearby Lawn Road, in the Isokon flats, built by Wells Coates. They were frequent visitors to the Mall, as was Piet Mondrian, who came in 1938 to live at No. 60 Parkhill Road (where James Linton used to live). A blue plaque now commemorates Mondrian's stay there. The thirties were a period of intense and far-reaching artistic activity in the Mall Studios and the surrounding streets. It was, as Herbert Read said in *Apollo* (September 1962), 'a spontaneous association of men and women drawn together by common sympathies... and there was a prevailing good temper, an atmosphere in which art could grow'. In 1938 Alexander Calder, the American sculptor, famous for his mobiles, gave a performance of his 'Circus' in Cecil Stephenson's studio. This consisted of wire sculptures with wood and cloth, of a simplified marionette character, based on his drawings from Barnum's Circus. This was the only performance he gave in England.

By the outbreak of war in 1939, most of the artists had left; only Cecil Stephenson remained. In 1940 Henry Moore was bombed out of 11A Parkhill Road and moved to No.7, which is still owned by his family. It was the end of an era and, as Herbert Read said, 'such a feeling of unanimity was never to exist again after the war, but English art had come of age. Within the next decade it was to become what it had not been for a century, an art of international significance'.

Since the war, the pattern in the Mall Studios has remained similar, with a quiet, harmonious atmosphere and long-staying residents.

constructive art edited by J L Martin, Ben Nicholson and Naum Gabo; and *Axis* (1935–37), with contributions by artists from the Mall and the surrounding area.

Henry Moore bombed out

During that period, Henry Moore lived in 11A Parkhill Road, and Moholy Nagy, the Hungarian avant-garde art-

First published in full in 1980 in Camden History Review No.8. *Reproduced by courtesy of Camden History Society.*

Henry Moore in his studio at 11A Parkhill Road in about 1934.

THE HENRY MOORE FOUNDATION

NEW STUDIOS, THE MALL, PARK ROAD, HAVERSTOCK HILL

from The Architect, *17th August 1872,"Works in Hand"*

A range of eight studios, seven in a group, and one detached, are in course of erection on ground adjoining the garden of the priory of St Dominic. Each studio is 25 feet by 20 feet, and about 20 feet high to the ridge, and has small waiting-rooms, costume-rooms, lobby, and other necessary conveniences. The light is from three skylights in each, in addition to a large window with a north-east aspect. The walls are of red bricks from Messrs. Culverhouse, of Hampstead; the roofs, of open timber construction, varnished but not stained, are covered with red tiles from Messrs. Seeley, of Bridgewater; and the chimney-pots of similar materials, specially designed with incised ornaments, and bearing the monograms of the respective owners, were made by Mr. Cooper, of Maidenhead. The lintels to all the square-headed external doors and windows are of American hickory. In the chimney breasts and recesses for cabinets, the red-brick facing is left exposed, these openings having pointed arches in moulded bricks. The shelves and moulded corbels to the chimney-pieces are in Portland stone. Where the brickwork does not appear the walls will be plastered up to the wooden moulded cornice at the plate-level, and the dado, coloured dark, about 8 feet high, will serve as a background for pictures.

Calorigen coal stoves, manufactured by Messrs. Farwig & Co., of Queen Street, will be used in the studios, the costume-rooms being fitted with wrought-iron Kentish cradle grates, the hearth and also the entrance-lobby paved with red tiles. The joiners' work is all planned, and the mouldings worked out of the solid; and the windows, except the large ones in the studios, will be glazed with old-fashioned crown bulls-eyes. The cost of each studio will be from £325 to £350. Mr. Eddy is foreman of works; the architect is Mr. Thomas Batterbury, of 106 Cannon Street, City.

The studios are for the following artists:– Messrs. R. Macbeth, E.F. Brutnell, A.S. Coke, E.J. Gregory, J.D. Linton, W.B. Morris, B. Montgomerie Ranking, and Thorne Waite. Eight more studios will shortly be erected in the same neighbourhood.

An aerial view of 1961 showing The Mall Studios (lower right, behind the houses of Parkhill Road). Above and to the left is St Dominic's Church and, at the top, the St Pancras Almshouses. AEROFILMS LTD

Editor's note: This extract appeared in the 1986 edition of this book.

MOVING INTO THE MALL STUDIOS

Lady Read talks to Leonie Cohn

LR We first met Gabo some time during the war. We hadn't any black-out material, and so when he came we had to sit in darkness, and he came and he and Herbert began talking at seven; and I woke up at twelve and they were still talking.

LC Where was that?

LR At Broom House – in Bucks.

LC But I thought you had met Gabo a long time before, when you were living in the Mall Studios.

LR Never.

LC Do you remember the Mall Studios?

LR Oh a lot, a tremendous amount, yes.

LC Do you remember when you first went there? When you first set foot in it – you weren't living there then.

LR I suppose we must have gone to visit Ben and Barbara, but at that time we started married life, more or less married life, in Henry Moore's flat which he lent us, in Parkhill Road. He was the only man who had any money in those days. He had £300 a year because he taught, and he lent us, and I remember practising my violin or viola or whatever it was in a room with all his little early wood carvings: one specially of a little figure that I always longed

to own; but of course we had no money in those days and we never thought of possessing anything.

LC Was he actually working in that studio?

LR They must have been on holiday, I think. Certainly he was normally working there because all his works and tools were round about.

LC And then how come you moved into the Mall, how did that happen?

LR We met Barbara and Ben, and Herbert was the only one who could write about them and he immediately became friends and wrote about them. He was really the spokesman of that movement, of modern art and abstract art and they loved him; and they used to come and talk; they lived in number 7, and they found that another number – three – was vacant and we went in there.

LC The very first time you saw the studio can you describe it?

LR Well, it was in rather a sort of more commonplace part of Hampstead, and you went up a little path which I didn't like because it was slightly smelly – you know, smelly greenery, London greenery, which I didn't like very much, and then you went inside those little doors and there was this huge lovely room in front of you, with a huge window,

Editor's note: This article appeared in the 1986 edition of this book.

Ben Nicholson, about 1933.

a little garden outside and a monastery garden beyond. There we were.

LC You must have had to find some furniture – you had nothing, didn't you?

LR We got one of the lovely steel chairs, a black Breuer chair and we had a beautiful stove which we got rid of later, I am sorry to say. And then Ben came in with a picture which he hung above the stove.

LC How nice of him...

LR Yes, that was very nice – and about half an hour later he came back and he said the distance between the top of the picture and the ceiling is too great and in his hand he carried, wet, a red circle, and inch by inch Herbert and he moved it up the white wall until they found the exact place for it to stay and so there it stayed.

LC The red circle was a piece of painting?

LR It was a painted circle, flat – and he carried it in wet, and then – there must have been a ladder, I suppose, because it was a very high wall... and what else: oh, I know what we got – we got a white skin sofa, very large and very grand; and then we covered the floor with almost white linoleum.

LC Where did the sofa come from?

LR It was from a furniture shop off that road that goes behind Regents Park up to Camden Town, there was a special modern furniture shop which made it for us, and there was an armchair as well, to match. The rest of the furniture was Aalto furniture. We had a round table, with a round cover, covered with linoleum and rather nasty little chairs, plywood stools; you always tripped over them.

LC And then you had a bedroom? Or was it all in the same room?

LR There was one studio and a stair going up, and at the top a sort of covered platform where we slept; and then, off the main room was a little room where my German friend Munza Braunfels slept and a little kitchen and a little lavatory. What did we have for a bath?

LC Perhaps you didn't?

LR Oh indeed we did, Herbert was very proper.

LC Were the Lawn Road Flats built yet when you moved in?

LR No, I remember them going up – and they looked very pretty because they were painted white. And then you see people like Gropius lived there and Adrian Stokes – in the Lawn Road Flats. And the little man who had them built.

LC Jack Pritchard and Molly.

LR Jack Pritchard, he lived there as well.

LC And you went and visited there too?

LR Oh yes we went and visited them. I remember having something like rook pie, which I didn't like at all. There was a kind of cookery club connected with it. I remember, Gropius coming and being very nice. Only, what disturbed me so much was that he talked broken English so that to me it was baby talk – and I couldn't bear to hear it, but as soon as one talked to him in German, there he was himself.

But this baby talk from an 'Ulanen Officer', which is what he had been, I found very distracting.

LC He was very upright, in all senses, wasn't he?

LR He was very kind, and very funny too. He said he remembered when he first came, that sign 'Take Courage', and he thought how wonderful it was that the English should be so moral that they had huge advertisements saying 'Take Courage', long before he realised that it was for beer. She, Isa, was very nice and very good-looking and very on the spot, and always had her hair platinum blond.

LC When did you meet Adrian Stokes for the first time?

LR Well, when he first came to the Lawn Road Flats. I didn't like him at all; I was very shocked because he had a gal staying with him when he wasn't married to her. At the time I wasn't married to Herbert; Ben wasn't married to Barbara – Margaret Gardiner was married to... Nobody was married, and to me – I found that terribly shocking; I was really a great prude. And so I didn't like him very much. People found him beautiful. He had enormous wide eyes, which went nearly to the back of his head. His relation with Herbert was very funny; because Herbert had used him as an illustration in one of his books – I think *Style in English Prose* – for 'how not to write', but later he became very great friends with him, and I think admired him quite a lot and they got on very well, so that he had rather changed his tune.

LC Did he resent this fact that he had been used?

LR Not at all; he adored Herbert. Nobody could have resented anything that Herbert did. Because he was very – you know, soft-spoken; in fact didn't speak very much at all.

LC Did Ben Nicholson talk about his earlier work?

LR He told us that he had painted people's portraits and

Henry Moore's hands and one of his carvings, 1934.

PHOTOGRAPH BY THEA STROVE, THE HENRY MOORE FOUNDATION

that he was specially good at pearl necklaces – and then overnight he broke off – I think because of Picasso, and everybody was dead against him, and then he met Barbara Hepworth and he just went along to the house and just took her away.

LC She was married to John Skeaping, of course.

LR Yes.

LC Had she already become abstract by then – or did she change too, overnight?

LR I don't really know. She did a beautiful sculpture of her pigeon. But I think that was when she was still at college. I don't know; at any rate they both became abstract together.

LC Did you go and do your shopping in Haverstock Hill? I mean how did you keep house?

LR No, we went through the Priory; there was a little passage, and if you went to the Priory and said one prayer you nipped out at the other end and there you were

in Kentish Town and, I think, that's where I did most of my shopping.

LC Because it was cheaper, I suppose.

LR And it was also much, much nearer. And there was a movie there, just opposite the passage. You said a prayer, nipped out of the church and into the movies.

LC Was it a pure fluke that you, a Roman Catholic, were so close to a Catholic church?

LR Oh, a pure fluke.

LC That was extraordinary, wasn't it that you had it really all laid on.

LR It was very nice and there was the Monastery at the end of our garden, a long, little garden.

Who's who

The late **Lady Read** (Margaret Ludwig) was a musician, one-time member of Glyndebourne Orchestra and the widow of Sir Herbert Read. Lived in Mall Studios 1934–1938.

Naum Gabo, Russian-born constructivist sculptor who lived in England throughout the war; went to America, where he died in 1977.

Ben Nicholson, celebrated British abstract painter and sculptor, married to Barbara Hepworth.

Barbara Hepworth, Yorkshire-born sculptor. First married to sculptor John Skeaping, with whom she lived in the Mall Studios from 1927.

Alvar Aalto, Finnish architect-designer whose furniture was sold in the thirties in London through Finmar.

Adrian Stokes, painter, writer, ballet enthusiast and author of several works including *The Stones of Rimini*, *The Rough and the Smooth* and *Invitation to Art*.

81

THE MAKING OF THE LAWN ROAD FLATS

Beginnings

Wells Coates[1] had a very very strong personality, we were somewhat bowled over by him. In many ways it was most fortunate that Molly became very fond of him, because Wells was difficult to deal with. We had bought a piece of land in Hampstead, and we were thinking of having a house built, and the first attempt at getting a design was not what we wanted. And then we immediately got Wells to start off, and to make some suggestions for a house. And while those discussions were going on, Molly began saying, isn't it rather wrong of us to have one house on this lovely piece of land: oughtn't it to be a multiple house, a block of flats? And Wells Coates came in and said, yes, of course, that's what I always thought all the time – but he didn't actually say so at first. Who was it who said it was Wells who told us to have a block of flats? no, it was the three of us in talks together; no particular person, I think, had the full merit of making that decision. At one point we were thinking of having standard small houses that we could begin marketing, and that seemed to be financially easier than the block of flats. Now that's where we had a bit of a difference of opinion, because Wells wanted to have the flats, and we wanted at least to have those plans for houses at once, so we might be able to sell some to help finance the rest of it.

But eventually we came to terms with Wells, and the flats were winning. And when we saw the first plans we were completely and utterly convinced that it was right to do it. They were first-rate plans, the whole thing was very beautiful. But how to finance it – I was just in a state of bewilderment, I didn't know how we could finance it. Molly and I between us, I suppose, could find four to five thousand pounds if we really tried.

At that time, that would be about 1932/33, there were proposals for a modern design exhibition at Dorland Hall – modern British design – and the architect Maxwell Fry and Wells got together and said, why don't we show a full-scale replica of one of the minimum flats in Lawn Road? That would make first-rate publicity for us. It seemed to me straightforward good marketing: instead of building the building and then going to a house agent to try and let the flats, there we were at Dorland Hall; the building hadn't been started, but we started trying to sell flats then and there, getting deposits. Out of thirty-odd flats we sold leases for about twelve: I was disappointed, yet that was the thing that made the whole success of it. It was a very good exhibition, and it gave us an awful lot of publicity.

1. Wells Coates (1895–1958), engineer, architect and designer

Jack Pritchard

Editor's note: This article appeared in the 1986 edition of this book.

Meanwhile we had got introduced to a solicitor who was able to put up building finance; for building finance you had to pay more money down than you would for a mortgage. Well, we had to produce a certificate by the architect, every fortnight I think it was, for a couple of thousand pounds, and each time we presented it there were extras, and I felt I was getting caught. Now, fortunately the Design and Industries Association had made me chairman for a year, and I had on my committee the great Frank

Left: Wells Coates' isometric drawing of the flats was used on the cover of the brochure used to sell them. Pritchard recalled, '...Coates often used isometric perspective... so 'isometric unit construction' became 'Isokon'.

Above: The marketing of the Lawn Road flats: an advertisement of 1934.

THE PRITCHARD PAPERS, UNIVERSITY OF EAST ANGLIA

Sliding doors show the Japanese influence on Coates' work, as well as the ingenious pursuit of space-saving solutions.

Pick[2]. He was splendid; he gave me lots of good advice. And when I told him about my trouble with the finance he said I was a silly young man and I should get rid of the finance people as soon as I could. The result of that was that I acted too soon, and I had a mere fortnight to find the money. But once more I had tremendous luck. I was introduced to the District Bank, the Manager of which said much the same as Frank Pick did. Didn't I know that we were only just beginning to climb out of a very bad slump? And that a lot of flats were standing empty? But when I showed him that we had already let twelve flats, with deposits paid, he was very startled. I said, come and see the building. And when he saw it and clambered over it – it was then about four and a half feet high – he came back and immediately said he would let me have the money on ordinary bank loan. The relief was quite terrific.

The character of Wells Coates

Wells was a fascinating person, I had never met anyone quite like him before. It was difficult to find out from him a lot of specific things. For instance, was he an architect? Had he an architect's training? No, he hadn't. Had he done buildings before? No. He never actually said no to that question. He was, of course, an engineer. He

2. *Frank Pick (1878–1941) was General Manager of London Transport, and a great patron of the best modern design.*

The Isobar, designed by Marcel Breuer – note the furniture. The map on the wall is of Hampstead.

THE PRITCHARD PAPERS, UNIVERSITY OF EAST ANGLIA

not only had got his degree as an engineer, he got a PhD [for a thesis] on the gas flow of a turbine. It was Sherban Cantacuzino who wrote in his monograph on Coates 'that gave him an edge, an intellectual edge over many of the other young architects of that time'. His engineering and scientific knowledge was pretty sound. He had come to England from Canada; he had been in the British Air Force. He had a lovely motor car, a Lancia, the last word in design. He was born in Japan and he was very interested in the Japanese scene. And in the flats, particularly in the ones on the south side, there is just the beginnings of the flavour of the kind of part-itions that the Japanese had, only in our case they were much heavier.

The coming and going of Gropius

In the early thirties I was beginning to be caught up with the Bauhaus, and I began to realise what a chap Gropius must be. I was introduced to Morton Shand, a writer. His family were concerned, I think, with a factory making velvet in Lyon. He had understood the situation in Germany, he had understood the significance of Walter Gropius and some other architects – Le Corbusier for one – and he realised the danger that Gropius himself was in. He was more or less bullying me to do something about it. At lunch one day he asked how the flats were getting on, and I was complaining that we had not yet let them all, though we had made a good start. "So you've got vacancies," he said. "And what about doing something

Isokon in its prime.

THE PRITCHARD
PAPERS, UNIVERSITY
OF EAST ANGLIA

about Gropius?" Well, I was a young man of about thirty, and who was I to ask, or even think of asking such important people.

Anyway, that was the beginning. Had it not been for Morton Shand, I don't think I would have had the courage to ask Gropius – it wouldn't have even occurred to us. So when Gropius came in 1934 in June for the RIBA exhibition of some of his work, I met him for a moment, but Maxwell

Fry immediately offered him a partnership, which was just what Morton wanted. I and Mollie offered accommodation free, and food, for as long as was necessary.

Then, of course, before Gropius could come he had to be assured that there was work for him to do, and work that he could start on at once. We found two very good possibilities, one in Birmingham and one in Manchester. But how could we get him out? Gropius was in Berlin.

Well, Nazi Germany and Fascist Italy were allies, so it wasn't too difficult to get a return ticket from Berlin to Rome and back. So he left his flat on a temporary basis – as if he meant to return – and off he went to Rome. There he managed to get his ticket adjusted, and came to London. Fry, Morton Shand and I met the train at Victoria Station on the 18th October 1934 – and out of the train came not only Gropius but a perfectly magnificent girl, Isa. I didn't know he had married again, and we had only arranged a tiny little flat for Gropius, because the building wasn't finished. So I told Max and Morton to keep them chattering on the platform, telephoned Molly and said that some-how or other we had to find some more furniture for a slightly bigger flat. And that's briefly how Gropius came to England.

The flats and their inhabitants

The flats, of course, were splendid for Molly and me; even if we were short of money, we wouldn't have to pay rent, and we could get meals and could entertain in our little club. Now, the club is interesting, because when we were working out the original scheme, before the building had started, we had thought of having – I think it was probably Wells's idea – a miniature restaurant. But we took advice and we decided, no, it's too risky. We had taken quite enough risks as it was. But after the flats had been going a little while, and we realised that the accommodation for the staff and for the meals that we were ready to deliver to people's flats was too extravagant, we decided to turn it into a little club and a restaurant. Meanwhile Marcel Breuer, the Bauhaus designer and architect, had followed the Gropiuses to London and into our flats, and we asked him to design the club-cum-restaurant for us. I don't think that Wells was very pleased about that, but he took it very well. Breuer did a delightful scheme: we had a nice little club room, with a bar and a tiny restaurant.

The life at Lawn Road was quite remarkable because, for some reason or other, even before the Isobar, there did seem to be a community feeling. But when we had the Isobar it very definitely came to life; and particularly during the war. Fascinating people stayed there. For instance, right at the beginning, one of the first tenants was Nicholas Monserrat, the novelist. Later on during the war, Agatha Christie and her airman husband; then we had another Bauhaus teacher/designer for a short time, Moholy Nagy, and Breuer for a short time. But as for Walter Gropius, in the end we failed to provide him with work. We still believed that, now that he was in partnership with Maxwell Fry, installed in London, surely jobs would flow into his office, but we were just wrong. England was too slow, and the only sizeable work that he and Max Fry achieved was that very remarkable building and social experiment, Impington Village College in Cambridgeshire. So when he received an invitation to go to America, he just had to accept it.

Of course I wanted to have a big farewell dinner party for him, and I went to see Bobbie Carter, who was the Librarian at the Royal Institute of British Architects, and he more or less took it over and arranged an RIBA dinner. It was a grand affair: H G Wells was there, Julian Huxley in the chair, and all sorts of people. Of course, great things were said about Gropius, there were fine speeches, but one couldn't help feeling that among some of the architects there was an underlying sense that 'yes, we recognise what an important man he is, but wasn't it rather fortunate perhaps that he was going away, and would no longer disturb our status quo?' That, at least, was the feeling Molly and I were left with at the end of that dinner party.

JACK PRITCHARD, A DESIGN CLASSIC AND THE (SECOND) MOST UGLY BUILDING IN ENGLAND

An archivist's view of the creator of Isokon

The voluptuosity of paper and ink that is the stereotypical archive takes people in different ways. They incline either towards slash-and-burn, or to sequestration in hallowed seclusion, where, like one of those giant subterranean fungi, the hoard threatens to occupy vast territories by stealth.

Well, up to a point. In practice, the vagaries of living – and the longer the life, the more of them there are – determine what survives and what does not. The Pritchard Papers are the surviving documentary records of one many-faceted life.

The archive is a mixture of voluminous detail, frustrating lacunae, the trifling, and pure gold. From it we know something of how Jack Pritchard raised the money to build the Isokon flats in Lawn Road, Hampstead. We know that client and architect had a falling out (don't they always?). We have a model of the building (somewhat battered). We know about leaking roofs, defective finishes and temperamental central heating. On the other hand we have scarcely any drawings.

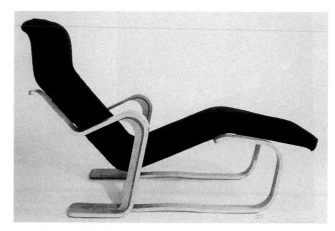

Breuer's Long Chair.

THE PRITCHARD PAPERS, UNIVERSITY OF EAST ANGLIA

Similarly, we have many letters describing the way that Marcel Breuer's famous long chair was modified time and again between 1936 and 1938 (I doubt if there is such a thing as a definitive version), but very few of the sketches

Deirdre Sharp

Curator of Archive Collections, University of East Anglia, Norwich

or blueprints that accompanied those letters. Some, we hope, have survived among the working records of the present makers of the chair, Isokon Plus.

So who and what was Jack Pritchard?

Good question; it's difficult to say exactly. Alastair Grieve, in his introduction to *The Pritchard Papers*: a guide, records that Jack would describe himself, 'mischievously', as an entrepreneur. Jack's surviving son, Jonathan, might frown if this description were to be taken too literally. Diana Rowntree called him 'a catalyst of design'[1], but he clearly was changed himself by the reactions that he brought about. The current term 'facilitator' is inadequate as well as ugly. He was quite simply the man who made things happen, often against the odds.

John Craven Pritchard was born in Hampstead on the 8th June 1899, at 6 Compayne Gardens, an area that he described in his autobiography as 'the less fashionable side of Finchley Road'. He was the youngest of the four children of Clive Pritchard, who was a barrister and the son of a solicitor, and his wife Lilian. In 1902, the year that Clive was elected Mayor of Hampstead, the family crossed the Finchley Road to the distinctly more select Maresfield Gardens.

After prep school, Jack went to Oundle in the footsteps of his brother Fleetwood, five years his senior and throughout their lives something of a hero to him. Subsequently both went up to Cambridge, to their father's old college, Pembroke, but not before they had suffered the loss, first of their father in 1914, at the early age of 51, and then of friends in the Great War. Fleetwood went to the front, and Jack, after a cadetship at Keyham Naval College, Devonport, served on HMS Lion for the last year of the war.

It is tempting to speculate that Jack's enthusiasm for modernist design was influenced by the orderliness, economic use of space and functionality of shipboard life. He certainly seemed to have appreciated at a young age that continentals were rather smarter than the British when it came to home comforts; in his autobiography he describes, with some admiration, the large stove that Belgian refugees lodging with his widowed mother had installed in the hall.

Jack read engineering at Cambridge, and it was here that he made many life-long friends, and met his future wife, Molly Craven, then a medical student. Molly apart, three Cambridge personalities whose influence on him was to be significant were a couple of dons, Mansfield Forbes and Philip Sargent Florence, and Henry Morris, then secretary to Cambridgeshire Education Committee.

After Cambridge Jack had difficulty in deciding on a career, but eventually fixed on industry, and joined the Michelin Tyre Company as a management trainee. Then an unfortunate misunderstanding over what Jack took to be the offer of a good job elsewhere left him, in 1924, unemployed – and on the brink of marriage.

Jack and Molly Pritchard were married in August 1924, and set up home in Belsize Park. Their two sons, Jonathan and Jeremy, were born in 1926 and 1928 respectively.

Rescue from unemployment came in the form of Venesta Ltd, importers of plywood and manufacturers of plywood goods. Venesta put Jack in charge of advertising – which was also Fleetwood Pritchard's line of business – and marketing. Among his tasks was the identification of new markets for plywood, and it was through Venesta that in 1929 Jack met the young Canadian engineer and designer Wells Coates. Coates was then designing interiors for Cresta Silks' shops and their Welwyn Garden City factory, exploiting the distinctive character and qualities of plywood to realise his designs.

1. Diana Rowntree, architectural historian and writer on architecture and design: 'The Ideal Client', The Manchester Guardian, *26th September 1963.*

Isokon from the air, May 1963.

AEROFILMS LTD

During 1929 and 1930, Jack made several visits to France on behalf of Venesta, and there he saw for the first time examples of the work of Le Corbusier, his cousin Pierre Jeanneret and Charlotte Perriand. Bowled over, he persuaded Venesta to commission the trio to design the company's stand for the 1930 Building Trades Exhibition in London. Subsequently Venesta's trade stands were to promote the work of Coates and Berthold Lubetkin.

By now Jack was positively fizzing with enthusiasm for modernism, both the style and the inextricably linked philosophy. He, Molly and Coates together founded a design company, Wells Coates and Partners Ltd, and, with Serge Chermayeff (with whom Coates was designing the interior of the BBC building in Portland Place), Howard Robertson and Mansfield Forbes, formed the Twentieth Century Group. In 1931, Wells Coates, Jack Pritchard and Chermayeff went to Germany, where they met Eric Mendelsohn and visited the Dessau Bauhaus. By the end of the year the design company had become Isokon Ltd.

At around this time, Jack and Molly Pritchard bought a plot of land in Lawn Road, initially with the aim of building a house for themselves and an adjacent nursery school where their 'advanced' views on education could be put into practice under the direction of Beatrix Tudor-Hart. Beatrix was by then, coincidentally, the mother of Jack's daughter Jennifer. The plan for one house developed into a scheme for a group of houses, and then into the design for a block of flats. Wells Coates, sizzling with

'...a blaze of publicity': the opening of the Lawn Road Flats. The lady in the large hat may be Thelma Cazalet MP.

PHOTOGRAPH BY
EDITH TUDOR HART,
THE PRITCHARD
PAPERS, UNIVERSITY OF
EAST ANGLIA

enthusiasm for workers' flats designed by Walter Gropius that he had seen in Germany, was to be the architect. Coates was antipathetic to conventional notions of property, and summed up his scheme as providing 'a place which every actor in this drama can call his own place, and further than that my idea of property does not go'.

Molly Pritchard drew up the specification. The worker-occupants she had in mind were distinctly white-collar. A draft prospectus in the archive describes 'ready-to-live-in flats... designed for business men and women who have no

time for domestic troubles.' Everything 'unnecessary, ugly, inconvenient and "labour-making" has been eliminated, and yet everything essential is there, and is there in exactly the right position'. Tenants were expected to express their individuality with 'a favourite rug...books...a vase or two for flowers and perhaps a small table'. Beyond that, all that they had to provide were bedding and crockery. Bed and dining table folded up, to enhance the sense of space and light. Domestic troubles were to be taken care of by a 'competent maid' who would clean, polish and 'leave everything shipshape' each day, a manageress who arranged 'such tiresome details as laundry, mending and darning, and cleaning of suits'.

Building work began in 1933. In June of that year, at the Exhibition of British Industrial Art being held at Dorland Hall, Isokon Ltd exhibited a 'Minimum Flat' which was practically identical to the single flats being built at Lawn Road. A year later the flats were opened by Thelma Cazalet MP in a blaze of publicity.

Jack ventured to replicate the Lawn Road ethos, first in Windsor, then Manchester and finally in Birmingham (in the grounds of Philip Sargent Florence's large home in Edgbaston). The favoured architects were Walter Gropius and Maxwell Fry. Sadly, problems with raising capital and getting planning consents resulted in the abandonment of all of these enterprises.

Jack Pritchard's name is associated with two milestones in the history of modernism in Britain. One is the Isokon flats in Lawn Road, the other is the Isokon Furniture Company.

Until 1936, Jack remained in Venesta's employ. This provided him and his family with a degree of financial stability, and enabled him to develop his network of suppliers, manufacturers and designers, and to identify the potential markets for his company before risking all.

The furniture company had been set up in 1935. For several years, at Jack's prompting, Venesta had been producing modular shelf units designed by Wells Coates. Jack's new company assumed the marketing of these and products from other firms, such as Finmar and PEL. A showroom was opened in Wigmore Street. Isokon's resident designers were first Walter Gropius and then Marcel Breuer; Breuer's long chair has since become Isokon's 'signature'.

Isokon's heyday was the late thirties. World War II almost destroyed the furniture company (fortunately first John and Christine Webber of John Alan Designs and then Chris and Lone McCourt of Windmill Furniture kept the spark alive), and it certainly did for the original concept of the Lawn Road flats. In September 1939 the flats began to empty, as tenants were despatched elsewhere on active service or to civilian war work, or moved in with family or friends in safer locations 'for the duration'. Rent income evaporated, but the rates still had to be paid – and compulsory war damage insurance. The latter alone, at £200 per annum, absorbed the equivalent of the annual rent of a double flat, and there were only 32 flats in the block. Labour became scarce and more expensive, while food and basic household goods were either rationed or virtually unobtainable. Isokon's income relative to expenditure drifted further and further from Mr Micawber's definition of happiness. The post-war 'age of austerity' was inhospitable to the regeneration of a service economy, and times remained hard.

Before World War II ended, Jack was already being drawn into the planning of the post-war furniture industry, and it was this work that marked the second half of his career. He served as executive director and secretary of the Furniture Development Council from its inception in 1949 until his retirement in 1963, tirelessly promoting good design, quality and manufacturing efficiency. This remained his mission for the rest of his life.

In 1968, Jack and his family sold Lawn Road Flats to the owners of the New Statesman, believing them to be the most likely of several prospective buyers to manage the flats on something like their founding principles. Jack and Molly stayed on in number 32, their penthouse flat, until 1972. Letters that he wrote at the time reveal his distress at the decline, intellectual as well as physical, with which he felt that the neighbourhood was becoming infected.

Eventually Jack and Molly decided to move to their beloved East Anglia, a part of the country of which they had always been fond and a single-storey house –

The Bottleship, one of the Isokon Furniture Company's ingenious modernist designs.

THE PRITCHARD PAPERS, UNIVERSITY OF EAST ANGLIA

modernist to the last nail – in Blythburgh, Suffolk. Designed by Jack's daughter, Jennifer Jones, and completed in 1963, it is, of course, called Isokon. Molly Pritchard died in 1985, and Jack on April 27th 1992.

And the Pritchard Papers?

The term 'papers' is used loosely; the archive is a patchwork record of Jack Pritchard's life and of his businesses, made up of what he either chose to preserve or neglected to throw away. It is not vast, but its comparatively small scale belies its richness.

The archive began life in the School of Architecture at Newcastle University, where Jack Pritchard already knew Bruce Allsopp, then a senior lecturer. In retirement, when Jack was in demand as a speaker and began to write his autobiography, inevitably he needed to refer to his papers, and the shuttling of packages of files between Newcastle and Blythburgh was unsatisfactory for all concerned. For this and other reasons, relations soured.

In 1968, Jack and Molly had lent pictures and pieces of furniture to the University of East Anglia (UEA) in Norwich, for an exhibition. Subsequently they gave pieces of Isokon furniture to the university's fledgling collection of abstract art and design, and Jack gave lectures at UEA. The relationship blossomed, and in 1986, the papers were transferred from Newcastle to UEA, and are now in the University Library. Following the award of a major grant, they have archival-quality storage and are described in great detail in an online public access catalogue and a comprehensive illustrated guide, available both in print and over the Internet. Use of the collection has grown steadily, in no small part because of the current interest in the future of the Lawn Road Flats and the wider appreciation of the best of modernist design.

Lawn Road Flats and the Breuer long chair are good examples of the way in which you can reconstruct a 'life history' from the archive, and someone is already working on a Lawn Road 'family tree'. We know who lived there, and to an extent how they lived. It was frowned upon, for instance, to pick the flowers in the communal garden, or to do your own washing up if you had opted for full service

Life for the manageress could be fraught. Apart from fairly regular moans about the central heating, and routine reports of broken fitments or leaky taps, cockroaches attempted to establish squatters' rights from time to time. During the war, services could be badly disrupted, with dirty laundry uncollected and cleaning skimped. Occasionally there were allegations of theft. 'For months we have had to hide tea, sugar, jam, cigarettes and matches' wrote one tenant, Bruno Gans, in April 1942. He insisted on dispensing with service arrangements that were costing him £20 a year, on top of a rent of around £112 per annum for his single flat.

To accommodate the refugee designer and craftsman Naum Slutzky, who took on a second flat in 1944 to use as a studio – at the rent of £6 10s 0d a month – the bath was removed. Slutzky needed the space for 'important work'. He asked for the lavatory to be removed, too, but at this Jack demurred. For the novelist Agatha Christie the two adjoining flats that she rented, one for herself and the other for her secretary, were provided with a connecting door. At Lawn Road, incidentally, she was always Mrs Mallowan.

In the evolution of the Long Chair we see in the record how vision and technological and financial limitations met head on; how the design process followed a zigzag course, with customer and skilled artisan each making their contributions to the outcome. We know, in many instances, to whom Long Chairs were sold, the finish they chose, the upholstery fabric selected.

The greater part of the collection relates, not surprisingly, to Jack Pritchard's involvement in design and architecture, and to the various Isokon companies. There are also small but useful files of correspondence with leading figures in the worlds of design and architecture. Anyone researching the history of 20th-century design and architecture in Britain is likely to want to seek out archive material on Jack Pritchard and Isokon, and to turn up on our doorstep or, just as often nowadays, our e-mail. And inevitably there are documents relating to Jack Pritchard's family background, correspondence with or about members of his family, and social correspondence – invitations to dine, bread-and-butter thank you notes, chit-chat.

This social correspondence peaks during the war years, and again in the late 1960s and early 1970s. The material of the earlier period complements the files on the Isobar, the restaurant that Jack established in the flats, with Philip Harben as chef and manager, and the Half-Hundred Club, the dining club that usually met there. It is therefore possible to build up quite a good picture of this aspect of the social and cultural life of the area and the time. Diana Rowntree, who writes from first-hand knowledge, described the Isobar of the war years as 'a last-ditch HQ of good living'[2]. The later letters clearly arise out of Jack's work on his autobiography, and often recall earlier events and past times.

The archive highlights how, in different ways, the Second World War utterly changed lives great and small. The effect on the Isokon Furniture Company and the vision that bred the Lawn Road flats has been mentioned, but the war also gave Jack and Isokon unsung roles in providing asylum for refugees from fascism.

Jack had been a strident anti-appeaser, seeing the threats clearly and holding out a rescuing hand to his many friends and associates in Europe from the early thirties onward. The best known of these are Water Gropius, Marcel Breuer and Laszlo Moholy-Nagy, but there were many others. Employment by the furniture company became a means of securing precious work permits, and if this wasn't appropriate, Jack's friends and relations discovered a pressing need for domestic staff. Flats were made available to refugee agencies as temporary homes. The files that document all this make salutary reading.

More generally, the papers from the war period

2. Rowntree, ibid.

Jack Pritchard in his penthouse flat in Isokon, No.32, in 1972, displaying his legendary charm to a young museum assistant trying out his famous Long Chair.

PHOTOGRAPH BY
RICHARD SWORD,
COURTESY OF
GENE ADAMS

graphically illuminate life on the home front, in all its dislocation, deprivation, tedium and tragedy. Jack was too old for active service, and was consigned to the Ministry of Information's bureaucracy; his frustration is palpable. So is his distress at the death in action of a promising young architect, Tim Bennett.

A small series of files reflects Jack Pritchard's interest in sailing, particularly on the Norfolk Broads and other East Anglian waters.

Another series relates to his and Fleetwood's interest in film; this dates from the late 1920s. Recently Jack's son Jonathan presented the archive with a collection of 16 mm films from that time. Jack and Fleetwood established a

club, The Projectors, through which equipment could be hired, film professionally processed and screenings held. The club's secretary was Basil Wright, later to become an important figure in the British film industry.

Before his involvement with refugees, Jack's political activities were particularly directed to the planned economy. He was a founder member of Political and Economic Planning (PEP), now known as the Policy Studies Institute, and lays claim to coining its name. The archive contains good material on PEP's early days. Within a couple of years of the organisation's foundation in 1931, Jack fell out with it; with a group of kindred spirits, some from within PEP and others not, he published an alternative blueprint to the National Plan on which PEP was working. They called it *A View on Planning*, or, informally and tellingly, JAXPLAN.

It is worth mentioning two more series in the collection. The first relates to Jack's mentor and friend Henry Morris, an outstanding Director of Education for Cambridgeshire. It was through Jack that Morris provided modernism with a much needed leg-up when, in 1936, he commissioned Maxwell Fry and the recently-arrived émigré Walter Gropius to design the pioneering village college at Impington. Jack and Molly were among those devoted friends who oversaw Morris's medical care when his health broke down in his last years, and who established in his memory the Henry Morris Memorial Trust.

The other series is a small one, and consists of correspondence with Mansfield Forbes (a Cambridge don under whose influence Jack had fallen when an undergraduate), chiefly relating to the re-modelling by the architect Raymond McGrath of the interior of the house in Cambridge that Forbes had leased from Gonville and Caius College and re-named Finella. As with the Henry Morris files, there is poignancy here, for poor Forbes destroyed his health and fortune in creating Finella. This series is equally interesting as an example of the way snippets of history turn up in the most unlikely way. Another of Forbes' enthusiasms was the restoration to working order of Bourn Mill, the oldest surviving windmill of its kind in the country. Among the events organised to raise funds to buy and restore the mill was a series of open days at Finella, for which admission was charged. Wide publicity had been given to McGrath's innovative use in the house and its garden of glass, reflective surfaces (including a Venesta product, 'plymax', in which a thin metal skin was laminated onto plywood), lighting and water. Forbes went further and persuaded his friends Mr and Mrs Alfred Bossom to exhibit in Finella at the same time a new piece from their art collection, Jacob Epstein's *Genesis*. Apparently the crowds flocked in.

Finally, an explanation of the title of this piece. The design classic is of course the Isokon long chair. 'The (second) most ugly building in England' was the judgement on the Lawn Road flats of a poll of readers of Cyril Connolly's magazine *Horizon*, conducted in 1946. That verdict was, and is, grossly unjust. During the war the flats had experienced near misses and emerged battle-scarred. They had also suffered the crushing (but necessary) indignity of having their warm white walls covered with a liberal coat of camouflage paint. The Venus de Milo would look rough after all that. When the guide to the Pritchard Papers was in preparation, there was no hesitation as to what we would put on the cover: Lawn Road Flats, as restored around 1950 (almost) to its former glory.

SOURCES

Jack Pritchard, *View from a Long Chair. The Memoirs of Jack Pritchard*, London, Routledge & Kegan Paul, 1984.

Bridget Gillies, Michael St John and Deirdre Sharp, *The Pritchard Papers. A guide to the papers of John Craven Pritchard (1899–1992)*, Norwich, University of East Anglia, 1998. Copies of this 156-page illustrated printed guide to the Pritchard Papers cost £3 each, including postage and packing, and can be ordered from the Archives Department.

The Pritchard Papers are housed in the Archives Department of the University Library, University of East Anglia, Norwich. Access is free to researchers and interested members of the public free of charge. The Archive Department is open on weekdays between 9.30 and 16.00, except for Bank Holidays. It is helpful if anyone wishing to see the collection makes arrangements in advance, but this is not compulsory. The Archives Department is also happy to handle enquiries by post, telephone or e-mail, and can supply photocopies, photographs or scans of items, subject to their condition and confidentiality. Charges are made for these services.

ISOKON AND THE FUTURE

Isokon today.
PHOTOGRAPH BY
JAKE BROWN

Who knows what the future holds for the Isokon flats? Surely Agatha Christie's 'giant liner which ought to have a couple of funnels' has been beached on the shore of Lawn Road for long enough, enduring alternative periods of calm and storm while her ownership has changed over the years. She is now officially 'at risk', but she may be re-launched soon, and it is hoped that she will sail off into a secure and happy future under the flag of her new owner.

The London Borough of Camden, owner since May 1972, has now decided to sell the building. The heavy maintenance costs of such a pioneering structure, coupled with its Grade I Listing, have meant that any owner has to square the circle of keeping it watertight and habitable to present-day standards without destroying its unique

Gerry Harrison

*Isokon in about 1960,
when it was still being
well maintained.*

PHOTOGRAPH BY JOHN
MALTBY, THE PRITCHARD
PAPERS, UNIVERSITY OF
EAST ANGLIA

architectural detail. Wisely, Camden has now preferred to wish this onto others who can more easily bear the cost.

With this in mind, for the past year the council has encouraged its tenants to move out of Isokon, often to local properties where their connections with the area are retained. Some have been happy to leave. Others have left with a deep nostalgia for what was for so long their inimitable home, in spite of its troubles, which in recent years have included a suicide and a murder. Nevertheless, and despite attractive alternative property being made available to them, one or two tenants have found it difficult to move.

The block will soon be offered on the open market. It is at present designated in the council's Unitary Development Plan as Class Use C3 (that is, as a permanent dwelling). But there are some who would prefer it to be re-designated under Class Use C1 (for short-stay accommodation), on the assumption that this would encourage a more sympathetic range of purchasers. The argument is that, in the private sector, people may not wish to live permanently in Isokon, where the accommodation has obvious limitations of space for a resident of today, and where the Grade I Listing means that even minor alterations will have to be approved by the council and English Heritage. There would surely be those, however, who might be delighted to spend a couple of weeks or months in this world-famous block while visiting London on holiday or for work. It is also arguable that short-stay accommodation was among Jack Pritchard's original plans for his building. Many of the residents were invited to the Lawn Road flats (as they were then known) temporarily, including those friends of Pritchard who were expatriates from Germany.

A planning application was recently lodged by two amenity groups, the Belsize Residents' Association and the Heath & Hampstead Society, to change the Class Use to C1. It is rare for an applicant to have no intention of developing the property, and this example demonstrates the altruistic desire of local residents for a better future for Isokon. The application was lost on Appeal last June, but the applicants hope that this decision will not deter serious developers who have C1 Use in mind.

Camden Council has now registered over fifty expressions of interest in Isokon. It is proposed that a shortlist will be selected from those which, among other criteria, can demonstrate 'a commitment to and knowledge of the unique nature of this building'. At the time of writing, the marketing has not formally commenced, and there is still the opportunity for new bidders to register their interest through FPD Savills, the agents, in Hampstead.

A smooth sale may be complicated by the result of a condition survey by the architects Rees Bolter. This has identified that the building has suffered from structural movement at some stage. It is perhaps unconnected, but as far back as 1934 a tenant complained of jamming doors. An investigation is now continuing to determine whether this subsidence is historical or current.

It may even have been a result of certain difficulties during the design and construction process. In *The Door to a Secret Room*, Laura Cohn's fascinating memoir of her father, Isokon's architect, Wells Coates, she reveals the conflicts between Coates and Pritchard – both strong personalities – over fees, prices and schedule. The problems between architect and client may have contributed to a number of defects in the construction of what was, after all, a pioneering building.

In July 1930, Coates wrote to Pritchard: 'When you spoke with such enthusiasm of the plans for your house I was certain that one day we would be working together...' By April 1931, though, the optimism had faded, as Pritchard wrote: 'Therefore unless I get the impression that you trust me and that you are getting on with the job I shall pack up ISOCON (sic)... If the thing falls through it will be the greatest disappointment of my life'. Their relationship became stormy as the original scheme developed from a single house to two houses, to 'unit dwellings' and then to a block of flats – changes that obviously had financial implications for Jack Pritchard. In his book *View From a Long Chair*, Pritchard wondered whether the Lawn Road flats should ever have been built 'had I had the experience I have now, but with all the stupid mistakes I made I am very glad we took the plunge'.

The flats were advanced for their time. This was one of the first domestic buildings in the world to be constructed of reinforced concrete. Wells Coates angled its aspect to reduce the weight on the two nineteenth-century LMS railway tunnels underneath, but, instead of the cantilevered foundations that he originally designed to spread the load, the building has more straightforward pad foundations at a fairly shallow depth. The survey was unable to determine their design. The basement was flooded in 1934, and has remained so since that time.

The subsidence may have been caused by the inadequacy of these foundations, by the vibration of trains passing through the tunnels beneath or by tree root action. The clay excavated from these tunnels was used to level the ground on which Russell's Nurseries, now a housing estate, once stood, and much of it was also spread across the surrounding Hampstead fields. This uncompacted spoil may have contributed to the instability.

The result of the condition survey will have some impact on the sale price of Isokon, but Camden remains determined to sell the building. It is hoped that the settlement will not delay the disposal, because as the months pass the vandalism in the almost empty building increases and its fabric deteriorates.

The impending sale has attracted considerable press and media interest. Articles have rightly celebrated the years immediately after its opening in July 1934, the distinguished company of residents that Jack Pritchard attracted, and the conversion in 1936/37 of the kitchen and the housekeeper's rooms into the famous Isobar.

These stories have tended to ignore the flooding, the periodic leakage of rain through the roof, the breakdowns of the boiler, the 'shoddy finish' and the cockroach infestations during that time. The improbable sale to *The New Statesman and Nation* in 1969 indicated that Pritchard was unable to continue with what he calls 'the burden of responsibility' for the upkeep. A strange choice as landlord, the periodical divested itself of the building to the relatively new London Borough of Camden just three years later, but during its ownership re-converted the Isobar into three flats.

Camden's stewardship has not been entirely beneficial, and the intention to sell is welcome. Most architecturally damaging was the decision in 1984 to erect exterior heating pipes at the rear of the building. Their removal was demanded by English Heritage in 1998 in order that they should be re-introduced internally, but shortage of funds has not permitted this work to be carried out. It is expected that the priorities of any purchaser will be to deal with these heating pipes and to repair the building so that the long-term concerns of water penetration will at last be addressed. This restoration would also include the conversion of the three flats back into the Isobar as ancillary use for its residents, which should satisfy the council's planning constraints. With a sympathetic developer, Isokon could resume its place as an icon of modernist architecture.

If Agatha Christie ever returned to Lawn Road, she might soon see her 'giant liner', though now it is the equivalent of a rusting hulk, resplendent once again. She would also discover enough material among its designer, its owners and its 'passengers' to fill a dozen whodunnits.

A list of further reading on Isokon, kindly supplied by the author, can be found at the back of this book.

LOOKING AFTER WHAT?

Left: 'Sir Richard Steele's cottage, Hampstead Road.' Looking down what is now Haverstock Hill towards St Paul's. Mezzotint by David Lucas after John Constable RA.

CAMDEN LOCAL STUDIES ARCHIVE CENTRE

Above: The same view today. PHOTOGRAPH BY JASON SHENAI

I notice to my continuous astonishment that when a traffic refuge gets damaged, a road gang will be around in less than 24 hours to restore it. But should one of the bronze candelabra of Regent's Park Bridge be stolen or a charming fountain at Primrose Hill be vandalised, it will take years for the damage to be officially registered and, unless protest letters are written by residents, the fate of beautiful street furniture is often sealed. Usually it vanishes, and, rather than being restored or recovered, it is replaced by inferior objects which happen to be on the market.

Culture means – among other things – that certain objects and ideas are cultivated at a deliberate and regular pace, whether they be crops, monuments or mere advertisements. Standards and values are not given once and for all; they need to be nurtured; there has to be steady care and maintenance. Once the chain is broken, objects tend to deteriorate beyond repair. Examples abound of how even the highest values can in no time be trampled to dust, how the finest and seemingly most durable structures may wither away within a generation or two. To call

Leon Krier

Editor's note: This article appeared in the 1986 edition of this book.

Signs of neglect: unlike many garden walls, this one in Belsize Park at least retains its mouldings and balusters – but for how long? GLC ARCHITECTURAL DEPARTMENT

plan for a Westminster precinct) – if all these authorities had had their way, London would now be nearly unrecognisable. The West End would indeed have very little to envy the South Bank or Croydon, and Covent Garden would have become another – though publicly financed – Barbican.

Structural problems

I have lived in Belsize Park for more than ten years and have observed considerable changes at two different levels. Although it shows little on the surface, most family houses have gradually been converted into as many as five or even ten units. As well as the increasing urban through traffic, there is thus a growing density of population, of local traffic and of numbers of parked cars per house. Due to the large Victorian urban blocks, our area has relatively few streets, allowing only for a minimum number of alongside pavement parking spaces. The concentration of all types of school in the area (especially in Eton Avenue) creates traffic chaos twice a day, and the concentration of office development in Swiss Cottage will further exacerbate the situation. What I fear is that the pressure to build huge car-parks may one day become irresistible, which, in turn, will start a process of urban 'development' so typical of American down-towns and inevitably spelling urban decay.

The creation of 'protected' zones by means of road closures has had the opposite effect of the one intended. Instead of reducing traffic movement, it has encouraged it. Instead of reducing noise, pollution, wear and tear and accidents, it has increased their lethal effects on chosen areas.

I believe that the best way towards relieving these

something a 'conservation area' is a truism of sorts, for even an airport or a motorway spaghetti junction is in a sense a conservation area. Today, however, the concept denotes implicitly those areas where artistic and craft standards are threatened by commercial or bureaucratic ones, where aesthetic values come up against economic interests. The decay of the public realm and the expansion of the commercial/industrial bureaucratic dominion are undoubtedly related phenomena; thus the streets and squares of conservation areas rarely escape the damage caused by enforced public penny-pinching or ruthless speculative development; often the very authorities which are supposed to safeguard the environment become the agents of its decay.

If the Crown Commission (remember the Regent's Park Development scheme), if the GLC (remember the Covent Garden and Soho urban renewal projects and the rash of deadly post-war housing ghettos), if the Department of Transport (remember the metropolitan motorways projects), if government (remember Leslie Martin's pressures is through a change in planning policies, such as the gradual elimination of functional zoning. A more balanced distribution and mix of urban functions all over the district could help to recreate a more civilised urban life.

Aesthetic problems

Though the changing appearance of houses in a conservation area may not present as grave a problem as the structural changes I have described, it is nevertheless of central importance, not only to the houses themselves but to the streets as a whole. Painted stucco facades demand much maintenance, but each repainting can mutilate old buildings at least as much as heat or frost, if not properly carried out and supervised. It is not a question of ill will or capricious intent, but of professional shoddiness on the one hand and ignorance or lack of guts on the part of owners, local authorities, architects and builders, in that order.

The restoration of damaged, disfigured or missing architectural and decorative features (columns, cornices, corbels, capitals, dentils, balustrades and so on) costs only a fraction of the overall maintenance when calculated over several decades. It is, however, exactly the fine detail which decides whether a hundred-year-old building looks good or poor, and I consider it a government's and a council's duty to give financial incentives for the restoration of facades, gates, balustrades and other features in conservation areas. Rather than consent to further subdivisions and mutilation of houses, all authorities – including the government – should promote the integral restoration of those period features which link buildings such as we find in parts of the Belsize Area to their history. There are several ways of improving the situation at the local level. Years ago, Chester Council restored its city centre – and with it the spirit of the town – by setting aside a penny of the rates for conservation and refurbishment. Could not councils such

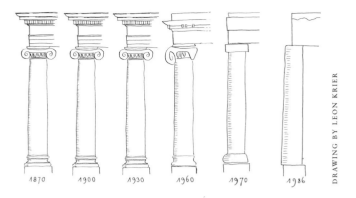

1870 1900 1930 1960 1970 1986

DRAWING BY LEON KRIER

as Camden do the same for us now? And at the government level, a system of tax relief for restoration and maintenance would make a real difference, as has been proved in the US where such a system has been in operation for some time; and of course the lifting of VAT on building restoration and maintenance work.

Aesthetic matters should transcend political interests; this is why their defence should depend on a personal involvement and sense of responsibility of those in authority. A change in direction can only come when local opinions – expressed through exhibitions and publications such as the present ones – will be heeded and acted upon at the highest level.

A HOUSE OF MY CHOICE

Having lived in Belsize Park for over ten years, I came to realise that the area has attracted a large number of other architects, many of them well known and distinguished, and including three British RIBA Gold Medallists: James Stirling, Norman Foster and Richard Rogers. It seems that the attraction of Belsize Park for architects goes beyond the purely practical, and, when it is compared with most other parts of London, probably has something to do with those basic architectural qualities, light and space.

Belsize Park is also at the centre of an area of Camden that has seen significant architectural achievement, particularly in public and private housing during the last twenty years. Many of these buildings were celebrated in the exhibition Modern Homes in Camden, presented by the London Borough of Camden Libraries and Arts Department in association with The Camden Society of Architects in 1984 as part of the RIBA Festival of Architecture. The achievement of the Camden Architects Department came largely as a result of Sydney Cook's appointment as Borough Architect in 1965, and of his ability to attract talented architects such as Neave Brown, Benson & Forsyth, Evans & Shalev, Peter Tabori and many others who were able to work creatively and productively to produce public housing of world class. The Fleet Road housing scheme, by Neave Brown, is an

example. Similarly, individual architects such as John Winter, Georgie Wolton, Michael and Patti Hopkins, and others, were also active during this time, and succeeded in building a number of distinguished single-family houses in and just outside the area. Examples of these are in Belsize Lane, Ornan Road and Downshire Hill.

The common thread which should unite both public and private housing is, first, the attempt to understand and come to terms with the real needs of urban housing at different scales; and then to answer these needs, without stylistic preconceptions, using appropriate technology in the most elegant way to achieve a high environmental, spatial and visual quality.

The pair of houses at 2C and 2D Belsize Park Gardens, by my own practice, is an attempt to build an oasis of light and space in a built-up area, and to produce houses that are economical, and versatile enough to answer the continually changing needs of expanding and contracting families. The problem was complicated by the fact that the site is in a Conservation Area, and the planning brief called for a five-storey block to match the existing buildings in the street. Although technically possible, a close match would have been financially impossible, with four-metre room heights and intricate mouldings, and the planners agreed that a single-storey development behind the existing

Robin Spence

Editor's note: This article appeared in the 1986 edition of this book.

2C and 2D Belsize Park Gardens.

PHOTOGRAPH BY ROBIN SPENCE

white screen wall would be in everybody's best interest. The houses more than satisfy the initial objectives by virtue of the constructional system and the plan form.

In the context of building in a Conservation Area, two courses of action are open to the architect: to design a visible building that attempts to set up an architectural dialogue with the surrounding buildings, by stylistic adaptation in some form; or to design a courtyard building (an ancient urban solution), in which the surrounding walls allow criteria involving quality of life to be con-sidered separately from external architectural constraints, so that the quality of environment is not compromised. Like the house at 34 Belsize Lane by Georgie Wolton, the houses at 2C and 2D Belsize Park Gardens adopt the courtyard approach. A visit to Georgie Wolton's house and the experience of living in my own are enough to convince me that the single-storey courtyard solution offers the more possibilities, in terms of quality of environment in a built-up area – I do not know of a house (in London) where I would rather live.

NEW BUILDING IN BELSIZE PARK

Change and conservation since 1985

Since 1945, Belsize Park has been something of a synonym for bedsit land, and since 1985 it has continued to grow in popularity with the young, as London itself has grown in popularity. But as the young have become more affluent, lodgings have given way to apartments. Many of the terrace houses close to Belsize Park Underground Station have been divided up into flats, interior styling has moved upmarket, celebrities have moved in and the whole area has become trendy. The wide pavements in Haverstock Hill, rare in London, give a French flavour to the terraces colonised by cafés on both sides. Wine and flowers are freely available, videos can be borrowed, the cinema offers a quickly varied programme, continental delicatessen is on tap, holidays can be booked, tennis can be played, and late-night shopping allows last-minute suppers to be offered even at the end of a strenuous day at the office. It is largely a yuppie scene. Summer in Belsize takes on a certain zest, and the Northern Line itself has shown signs of regeneration.

A little further out, other groups of shops, at Belsize village, at England's Lane and at South End Green (strictly speaking a corner of Hampstead) where the buses terminate, provide alternative destinations, a variety of restaurants and one of the last genuine butcher's shops in London. All of this renews our sense of London as a collection of villages, and makes the area one of the most attractive for permanent residents.

'...colonised by cafés'; the lively pavement life of Haverstock Hill.
PHOTOGRAPH BY CELIA SCOTT

But popularity brings problems, and exposes a certain opposition between the wishes of permanent residents, who naturally like things as they are and resist change, and the more mobile young, who are looking for excitement. The opposition appears in the long delay in redeveloping a few frontages at South End Green as 'food outlets', where these are perceived as a possible source of late-night disturbance. The same opposition shows up in the consolidation of the conservation movement and in the extension of the Conservation Area, and with every new intervention the planners are on the alert. So, paradoxically, new

C e l i a   S c o t t

Sarum Hall Girls School in Eton Avenue.

PHOTOGRAPH BY CELIA SCOTT

building in Belsize must learn to adapt to the context, become skilful at fitting in, and in certain cases, learn to be invisible.

This is paradoxical because Hampstead, to which Belsize has long been linked, has always enjoyed a reputation for intellectual distinction and progressive thought, and in the past has provided sites for progressive architecture. Maxwell Fry's Sun House, Cohn Ward and Lucas' house in Frognal and Erno Goldfinger's houses in Willow Road are now accepted as classic instances of the outrageous becoming acceptable. They are now part of the history books, and the recent construction of another white-walled villa in Upper Terrace seems to suggest that this tradition can continue. Belsize, too, may lay claim to some exceptional modern architecture. Wells Coates' Isokon block in Lawn Road is in desperate need of repair, and has raised the unexpected thought that a modern building that has become part of history may also require conservation. Little problem seems to attach to the two houses by John Winter in Ornan Road, which have stood the test of time

and are now part of the scene; and the discreet glass house built by Sir Michael Hopkins in Downshire Hill, thought by many to be something of a scandal at the outset, is now hardly noticed by the visitor as exceptional. The very beautiful house by Georgie Wolton in Belsize Lane has always been completely invisible from the street, and by now, with its wonderful garden, has matured into an idyllic piece of scenery.

Part of the trouble with new work is the sense of intrusion that comes simply from its first appearance on the scene, the mere fact of change; after an interval the new becomes familiar, and, through that fact alone, begins to 'fit in'.

So do not expect to find Belsize made over as a centre of new architecture. Recent buildings that serve social institutions can hardly be prohibited, but you must expect them to be as far as possible discreet, and pay respect to their neighbours. This is true in a very special way of the largest such project, the Sarum Hall Girls School in Eton Avenue. With its large slated roof it firmly continues the road frontage, which is anyhow softened by the mature trees, and makes a perfect neighbour to the nearby Edwardian villas. The use of red bricks is of course traditional in itself, but the architects (Allies and Morrison, 1994) have made a skilful use of some areas of white stucco, which, along with the tight handling of eaves and corners, imparts to the building a rather modern sense of precision and lightness. The white stucco, while it forms a lively contrast with the brickwork, also ties in with the white stucco gables or bay windows that appear frequently in nearby construction from the turn of the century, and with the many Victorian terraces that make up a large part of Belsize. The architects enjoyed the benefit of a spacious site, so that the plan can expand at the rear into a teaching wing. The school staff clearly enjoy the efficiency of the modern interiors, while appreciating the gentle way in which the building joins the community. There is real finesse here in the way the modern has been combined with the traditional, and the result appears relaxed and confident. To take one episode, the art room has been provided with a large north-facing window, very effective from within, but equally so on the outside, where its large dimensions are reduced to domestic scale by contrast with the dominating roof.

Not quite so successful is the new building for The Hall School, at the other end of Eton Avenue, at the corner with Crossfield Road. Here the architect (Shepherd Robson, 1995) wanted to create separate 'features' corresponding with functional divisions of the plan, so we have a curved corner block at one end and a circular brick tower at the other, both of which are given distinctive treatment. The curve goes well enough with the apartments behind it, and it makes sense to place these in Eton Avenue, but the circular tower houses both the main staircase and, at basement level, the kitchen, and here the link between form and content seems strained. Above, the staircase is

The new building for The Hall School, seen from Crossfield Road. PHOTOGRAPH BY CELIA SCOTT

rather monumental, while the kitchen below could do with being bigger: the kitchen staff are reduced to having their tea break in the adjoining basement car park. The gridded facade to Crossfield Road is softened by projecting shades, but these are hardly important for an east-facing aspect. Where Sarum Hall School makes an easy fit between inside and outside, here there is a more doctrinaire attempt to find a match between specific forms and the functions that they enclose. This was the original premise of modern architecture, but over the years we have seen the dogma in decline, and many excellent modern buildings are in no way compromised by a judicious separation of inside and outside, so that the exterior is freer to adjust to its setting. Further up Crossfield Road, the earlier addition to this school, with its 'rationalist' facade of regular win-

Above: The Hall School Centenary Building in Crossfield Road.

Right: The Central School of Music and Drama extension building, Eton Avenue.

PHOTOGRAPHS BY CELIA SCOTT

dows, shows how this can be done, and it is much easier to live with.

Nearer to Swiss Cottage, with its onrush of city scale, we have a recent addition to the Central School of Music and Drama (architects Cullum and Nightingale, 1997) which makes a clear virtue out of the separation of inside from outside. Inside we have many exposed concrete surfaces in structural walls and ceilings, neatly integrated with timber linings and floor coverings, all done with typical modern efficiency and precision. The toughness of the exposed concrete, with its connotations of workshop environment and back-stage intimacy, seems very appropriate for the purpose of the building as theatre workshop, studios and offices, and helps to create a purposive atmosphere. But none of this appears on the street, where a regular facade of vertical windows set in brickwork gives a distinctly

residential look, linking us with the Victorian terraces again. This is reinforced by the stone facing in the ground floor, answering to the usually stuccoed ground storey. The discretion of this building seems more successful than the earlier addition (by the same architects) on the Swiss Cottage side, which faces on to a rear courtyard, and is more aggressive in its use of a modernist vocabulary, as it does not have to worry about making appropriate noises.

Probably the new character which will be most visible to most local people is the work recently undertaken at the old Hampstead Town Hall (architects Burrell Foley Fischer, 2000). Six years ago, when this was a dilapidated heap, Camden thought of selling it off. Now it has been rescued by a combination of charity trusts in partnership with Camden Borough and the Friends of Hampstead Town Hall. Together they have been successful in

109

Above: The campanile of Hampstead Town hall: "a sort of cultural landmark, highly visible from Haverstock Hill".

Left: The Hampstead Town Hall's new extension, with the new atrium to its right.

PHOTOGRAPHS BY CELIA SCOTT

attracting support from the Arts Council and the Heritage Lottery Fund, as well as from private subscription. The Victorian building of 1877, with its Edwardian extension, has been thoroughly renovated and transformed into an arts and community centre, with an eye to preserving its considerable character. The campanile has been reconstructed from the original drawings and stands out now as a sort of cultural landmark, highly visible from lower down Haverstock Hill, and making the building something of a rival to the Camden Arts Centre in Finchley Road.

But the economics of development have also produced a considerable chunk of new building, in an extension that is set back from the street but still visible from Haverstock Hill. This part is an arts and media centre, with a dance studio and other completely modern facilities, and it has been designed in a clearly modern style, using a different treatment in the lower and upper storeys. The lower part is varied, partly by exposing the structure through a glass wall, partly by projecting a sort of 'landscape' wall that curves away freely from the building; while above, the main volume is picked out with a neat timber casing in the classic way first employed by le Corbusier, so that the building appears to be a crisp rectangle standing on stilts. The feeling is definitely abstract and modern, but it is done with some discretion, and the use of timber facing makes it quite polite. Not only is the new build-

(Above) Housing Association project at 126 Haverstock Hill, and its entrance (right).

PHOTOGRAPHS BY CELIA SCOTT

ing set back, but it is clearly subservient to the old building, and partly screened by a mature lime tree. It makes a decent space with the backs of the adjoining apartments.

Another case of a clearly modern building, on a more modest scale, is the new assembly hall which has been added to the back of Parkhill Day Nursery, visible only from neighbouring back gardens. The architect (Newton Architecture, with Barefoot and Gilles, 1999) has made a neat metal box with a curved metal roof and a glazed wall placed at a slight angle; from the outside it is decidedly under control, and its large windows look dutifully back to the parent building, making a nice space for the children's singing. It is quite hidden from the street.

In general, new development has not had as much visual impact in the Belsize area as one might have expected. The largest area of comprehensive redevelopment is on back land, next to the tennis courts behind the tube station, and only shows through its bombastic gateway on Haverstock Hill. There is nothing of recent years to match the massive redevelopment south of Adelaide Road which took place in the fifties and early sixties. Another case of back land development is to be found at 126 Haverstock Hill (a Housing Association project designed by Architype, 1993). Here two rows of houses and flats in yellow brickwork, arranged at right angles, look out on a piece of open space contiguous with the adventure playground in Parkhill Road, altogether forming an oasis of calm and a refuge for owls and urban foxes. These dwellings have been designed to work together in a modern version of the Georgian square, and are entirely unobjectionable. At the point where they connect to Haverstock Hill, a couple of apartments have been raised on cylindrical columns to act as a sort of gatehouse, rather more ostentatiously modern

The corner of Haverstock Hill and Parkhill Road.

PHOTOGRAPH BY CELIA SCOTT

which for anyone who loves architecture make it a charade. The concern to look traditional can be carried to absurd lengths, as with the residential block built opposite the Clive Hotel, which, with its excess of imitation period detail, provides an example of what might be called 'vernacular nook-and-cranny', at odds with the regularity and large-scale repetition of the Victorian terraces that make up so much of the Belsize area.

Conservationist policy must also be concerned with comparatively minor changes to the existing stock of buildings, and here there is a real problem, because of the increasing uncertainty produced by a wide-spread loss of job security. There are times when the only answer to a change in one's circumstances is to move: to a larger home when children arrive or a new job promises a more generous life-style; to a smaller one when the children leave home or a good job is lost. The higher level of property prices may well have discouraged many people from moving who would otherwise have done so. Whatever the reason, recent years have seen a notable increase in adapting to new circumstances by making changes in the house already lived in. Often this takes the form of building a new rear or side extension to provide a kitchen, dining room or other additional rooms; or roofs are extended by adding dormers, to provide additional bedrooms or make a loft. The number of such interventions must have been boosted by the popularity of television features on revamping interiors, and the increased sophistication of do-it-yourself remedies now available. The planners have to use their discretion in hundreds of such cases, weighing the gain in accommodation against the loss of original character or incompatibility with the adjoining houses.

in appearance. Coming at a gap in the Victorian terraces, this intervention was quite eye-catching at the time it first appeared, but by now its yellow bricks have rendered it quite innocuous.

Replacement of older buildings through piecemeal redevelopment has generally provided a handy way of taming the impact of the new. At the corner of Parkhill Road and Haverstock Hill, a substantial new construction (architects Pollard Thomas, 1994) has been contained within the volume of the large Victorian double house that it replaced. Although the detail, on inspection, reveals its recent origin, it blends with the adjoining houses by conforming roughly to their bulk and placement. In a similar way, a considerable piece of Elsworthy Road has been redeveloped as apartments, but again the new building is restricted in bulk to something close to the original, and the style is strenuously neo-Edwardian, of a kind, if we ignore the tell-tale indications of reduced storey heights and the proliferation of false chimneys,

Visibility from the street is an important consideration in applying a conservationist policy; visibility from the rear, usually divided up into a series of private gardens, is not so demanding, although the susceptibility of neighbours is sometimes a deciding factor. In cases of doubt, the planning authority has to take account of the weight of complaints. So it might be said that the architect Mark Guard was lucky to get permission for the extension he has added to a house in the Parkhill Conservation Area. This extension has a conservatory roof made of large sheets of plate glass which are both surface and structure, giving the naked effect preferred by the 'high-tech' architects who want the result to be exactly what it is – no more, no less. The result is uncompromising, but extremely elegant. Some discretion has been used, however, since the big area of glass is restricted to the roof structure, and the ground floor is screened by a white stucco wall that is an extension of the original house alongside. Seen from the garden, the new addition is not at all disruptive. The glass roof can be glimpsed from the street, but it would hardly be noticeable if you were not looking for it. The owner of this house has been meticulous in restoring it in all other respects to its original condition, in spite of residual war damage, with an 'authentic' front porch and real Corinthian columns, and every architrave lovingly restored. The partnership between old and new is highly successful.

Also extremely elegant is the glass front of a tiny extension to a house in Belsize Court Garages (The Architect's Practice, 1996), highly visible from the street just at the instant of passing it, but hardly offensive. It contains a living room, protected from intrusive visitors by continuous venetian blinds, the same system used by Hopkins in Downshire Hill, a system that in its own way has become a 'classic'. The declaration of modern style is muted by the fact that the building volume is respected and the facade is continuous with the Edwardian portion alongside. As often happens, the contrast is enjoyable in itself, and increases the appreciation of both styles of building. One would not want 'fitting in' to be applied so rigorously as to eliminate all contrasts of character.

There are no doubt other cases where a modern intervention has been permitted because it makes little

House extension in Belsize Court Garages.

PHOTOGRAPH BY CELIA SCOTT

tained, the swimming pool itself is to be replaced, and other recreational and commercial amenities are to be added, in a package that will also permit the construction of apartments. Local objectors are determined to save both Spence buildings, so the future of the scheme is uncertain.

However, this corner of Belsize Park is more vulnerable, as the corner on the edge of the area closest to Swiss Cottage and Finchley Road, a main artery from the centre of London and heavily trafficked. Here we are more at city scale, and the atmosphere is quite different.

Belsize Park itself is essentially a residential district, and its main street, Haverstock Hill, which leads directly to Hampstead, is a busy road, but not a principal artery out of central London. Less well endowed, perhaps, than Hampstead, which in Church Row has an enclave of true Georgian dignity, and in Flask Walk a corner of olde-world picturesque charm, Belsize is more and more visible as a district in its own right, more modern, more bracing, more convenient. In spite of its younger population, it has been largely protected from unsightly intrusions and metropolitan pressures. The work of the Conservation movement has surely contributed to this satisfactory condition.

or no public statement. Nicholas Boyarsky has designed a superb metal and glass extension to a house in Belsize Avenue, but it is invisible from the street, and largely screened by garden growth from its neighbours. Discretion has in general proved to be the better part of valour.

Great changes are bound to come with the redevelopment of the Swiss Cottage Sports Centre, probably to a comprehensive plan prepared by Terry Farrell Architects. In this proposal, not yet approved, while Basil Spence's library, with its distinctive vertical sunshades, is to be re-

THE RESCUE OF ST STEPHEN'S, ROSSLYN HILL

Early history

St Stephen's was built to provide an additional place of worship for the increased population in the Parish of St John created by the construction in the 1860s of new streets between Belsize and Hampstead, such as Lyndhurst and Thurlow Roads.

The land on which St Stephen's is built was donated to the Church of England as a gift by Sir Thomas Maryon Wilson, then Lord of the Manor of Hampstead. He would make later gifts of land in Pond Street for St Stephen's Hall (built as a school) and in Thurlow Road for the vicarage. The principal agents in these efforts were the Rev. Joshua Kirkman, minister of St John's Chapel, who would become the first vicar of St Stephen's, and Charles Henry Lardner Woodd, a leading member of Hampstead's new gentry, son of a wine merchant and resident of Rosslyn House.

The architect to the Church Commissioners, Ewan Christian, was a member of the congregation of St John's Chapel, and he was offered the commission, but he "graciously declined". The architect then chosen was Samuel Sanders Teulon, a successful member of the profession, although not in the mainstream of Gothic Revival.

Born of a Huguenot family at Greenwich on 2nd March

The tower of St Stephen's.   PHOTOGRAPH BY M L TAYLOR

M L Taylor

Chairman of the Trustees, St Stephen's Restoration and Preservation Trust

1812, he was the principal member of a group trying to create a new and modern architecture based on the Gothic style. They were known as 'Rogue Architects', and their work sometimes displayed eccentricity, although it was always vigorous.

Teulon's clients included Queen Victoria, the Archbishop of Canterbury, the Dukes of Marlborough and Bedford, and the Earl of Dulcie. Many of his buildings were churches, but he also designed almshouses, a number of major country houses, farmhouses and other estate buildings. A consistent theme through much of his work was the Gothic style of his designs, although Teulon was eclectic and freely experimented with the architectural fashions of the time.

In January 1866, Teulon submitted three alternative designs to the Building Committee, which selected one that took advantage of the sloping site to provide a crypt at the east end, below the apse.

The estimated cost of the church was £7,500, and the money was raised entirely by subscriptions and donations from local people, the prospective congregation. Apart from a few large donations, especially that from Charles Woodd, most of the money was given in units of £5 or £10, the equivalent of £1,300 or £2,600 today.

Work began in January 1869, and the church was consecrated within 12 months, on 31st December 1869, by the Bishop of London. Unlike so many Victorian churches, which remained unfinished for extended periods, St Stephen's was finished within three years of its consecration, with the clock and carillon installed in 1873. Within a year of completion, a school was established in the crypt.

Teulon's 'mighty church', as he called it, is markedly French in outline, with steep roofs and a massive square tower. When he was first offered the commission he had particularly requested that the church should be built of brick. For the exterior he chose hard brick from Dunstable

Part of the rich mosaic wall decoration of the interior.

PHOTOGRAPH BY ML TAYLOR

which, when new, was described as varying in colour from pale grey to Indian red, giving the church a mottled appearance. The decorative stone bands on the exterior were of Kentish Rag from Maidstone. In contrast with the exterior, the inside walls were faced with grey, yellow and white bricks from Huntingdonshire, laid in stripes and panels. The most spectacular ornamental brickwork is to be found under the tower and in the transepts, where it is distinctly Moorish in style.

In addition, the sculptural and mosaic decoration was unusually rich and varied. The nave capitals were sculpted by Thomas Earp, and the beautiful mosaics, the tesserae of which are still vibrant to this day, were by Salviati, a friend of Teulon. The alabaster roundels in the spandrels above the nave arches were added later, between 1880 and 1883, and were probably by Clayton and Bell.

Despite the rich decoration, St Stephen's was not intended for High Church ritual. Indeed, Ewan Christian gave the roundel showing Archbishop Latimer 'as a protest against Romanising practices within the Church of England'.

The stained-glass windows, many of them by Clayton and Bell or Layers and Westlake, were not all placed at the time of building. Some were donated in later decades, and the last was placed in 1914. In the south aisle was a memorial window to S S Teulon himself. He died of overwork in 1873, at the age of 61. His funeral service was held at St Stephen's and he was buried in Hampstead parish churchyard.

Recent years

St Stephen's continued in use as a church, with a good congregation, but by 1969 both the north and south aisles were affected by obvious cracking. Two independent surveys were made in 1971, on behalf of the Diocese of London and the Council for Places of Worship, but there was no agreement on the gravity of the defects. Accepting the more pessimistic views of their own surveyor, the Diocese united the benefice of St Stephen's with that of All Hallows, Gospel Oak. St Stephen's was declared redundant in May 1977 and closed for worship. In 1980 the building was placed in the care of the London Diocesan Fund.

Since then many schemes have been proposed for use of St Stephen's, ranging from the serious to the amazing, but none has come to fruition. This was because none has managed to convince all the various authorities concerned that it provided a suitable use for the building which would respect its fabric and character and would not create traffic problems, nor that the proposers could afford to restore St Stephen's and subsequently maintain it in the long term. At this stage no detailed survey was conducted by any party to identify the real cost of repairs.

English Heritage had by this time designated St Stephen's a Grade I Listed building, and they were very concerned that a user should be found who would repair and restore it.

In the course of over twenty years, St Stephen's has

The west wall, rose window and gallery.

PHOTOGRAPH BY M L TAYLOR

inevitably suffered some damage. All the stained-glass windows at ground-floor level have been stolen, and the lack of maintenance has exacerbated the mildewing of brick and stone, much of which was already crumbling from the effects of pollution.

A few years ago, shortly before its demise, the GLC funded some work to the roof, and this served to replace missing tiles, repair lead flashings and so on. It is likely that these roof repairs were critical in enabling St Stephen's to survive over twenty years of abandonment without suffering even worse damage.

In 1998, the Diocese of London, by now gravely concerned about the fate of St Stephen's, commissioned a Property Condition Report, with financial aid from English Heritage. The purpose was to identify the real prospective cost of repairing and restoring St Stephen's to a state befitting a Grade I Listed building. The figure appeared to be £1.2 million, plus VAT and design consultancy fees.

The Diocesan Surveyors then announced that any organisations which were interested in taking the lease and restoring the building should submit a properly detailed proposal. From these a scheme was chosen in December 1998, which had the approval of all concerned.

The future: St Stephen's Restoration and Preservation Trust

This trust was founded in January 1999, following the successful bid for the lease of the building, with the key object of restoring and preserving "for the benefit of the public the property known as St Stephen's Church ... and in particular ... to make provision for the use of St Stephen's for the purposes of education and for the benefit of the community of Hampstead..."

The London Diocesan Fund has offered the lease to the Trust on condition that the Trust grants a sub-lease to Hampstead Hill School, which is essential to provide a sound commercial income for the maintenance of the fabric of the building.

The Trust intends to restore St Stephen's to its former glory, repairing and restoring the fabric of the building to a sound condition, ensuring the repair of all decorative and architectural features, as well as replacing missing stained-glass windows and railings. This should enable the building to be reopened with an appearance as close as possible to the way it was before the war. Church and Hall will be re-united again on a single site, sitting amongst attractive gardens.

The existing crypt below the nave will be extended, providing an undercroft with six classrooms and facilities for the pre-preparatory branch of Hampstead Hill School, but no alterations will be made to the main body of the building. The Trust intends to replace timber screens around the choir and entrance as they used to be. The whole of St Stephen's at ground floor level will be available for community use.

The property will be managed by St Stephen's Restoration and Preservation Trust, the trustees and patrons of which are local residents who care about their environment and who are answerable to their own community as well as the London Diocesan Fund, the landlords.

The Lifelong Learning Centre and the Children's Museum

The principal use of the main body of St Stephen's, the nave and aisles, will be to provide a Lifelong Learning Centre. This will offer the teaching of post-basic reading, writing and numeracy skills, IT and computer literacy courses, language courses (including English as a foreign language), and life and social skills particularly designed for young people leaving care. It will also provide children's help-lines, with professional counselling.

In addition, St Stephen's will house The Children's Museum: a unique, hands-on, permanent museum of works of art in a variety of media, created by children for children of all ages and backgrounds. The Trust also intends to make the building available occasionally as a concert and performance venue.

St Stephen's is a very beautiful Victorian building, and of national architectural importance. It will now be open for the general public to visit, to see and to learn from, in all its glory as of old, yet looking forward to benefiting future generations.

BIBLIOGRAPHY

Neil Burton, *Greater London Council, Historic Buildings Paper No 1*

Teresa Sladen, Mathew Saunders and David Prout, *St Stephen's, Rosslyn Hill,* The Victorian Society (report, 1990)

THE RESTORATION OF HAMPSTEAD TOWN HALL

It is in the nature of things that most of the efforts of neighbourhood conservationists are on a small scale. So it is in Belsize, where causes – and successes – tend to be modest and accretive rather than spectacular. Nevertheless, as the millennium turns there are three important projects in the area. One, the rescue of the Isokon building in Lawn Road, hangs in the balance, but the optimistic watcher can perhaps detect a turning of the tide; there are ambitious plans for the rescue of St Stephen's, Haverstock Hill; but best of all, the restoration of Hampstead Town Hall has been completed, and the building is open for business, and for pleasure.

The history of this fine building and its rescue fairly represent the trajectory that many important buildings

Adrian Shire

follow, and the difficulties attending their conservation.

Before we had borough councils, the local authority was the parish vestry. That of Hampstead was originally based in the Parish Church of St John, in Church Row, but as its activities expanded it moved to progressively larger locations in the parish, and eventually to the dining room of the Workhouse in New End. Local parish vestries were reorganised in 1855, and the second half of the 19th century saw a huge growth in their power, activities and size. In 1873 the old parish of Hampstead was divided into wards, and the number of vestrymen was doubled to 60, necessitating yet another move.

In 1874, after much deliberation, Hampstead Vestry decided to build a new Vestry Hall, large enough not only to accommodate the needs of the Vestry but to be used for public meetings, concerts and other events. They therefore bought – from Robert Woodd of Hillfield, a mansion in Haverstock Hill – a quarter of an acre of land in Belsize Park, for £2,800. Both the site and the price were controversial. According to one correspondent, the land had previously been offered privately at a quarter of the price; and land values in the vicinity slumped soon afterwards, because of a proposal to build a smallpox hospital almost opposite.

A competition was held to choose the design of the building. Fifteen architects were invited to submit designs, eight plans were submitted, and a subcommittee whittled them down to three for the Vestry to make a final selection. At this point, however, the Vestry decided to consider only those proposals costing less than £10,000. As a result, two of the three finalists were replaced by designs previously thrown out by the subcommittee. The Vestry then chose the one that it considered the most suitable 'especially as to cost' – something over £9,000, according to the architects. This firm, which had submitted its scheme anonymously, was now revealed to be Kendall and Mew, of 30 Doughty Street, Mecklenburgh Square: which is to say, Frederick Mew, and his partner, HE Kendall, who was the Vestry's own District Surveyor. *The Builder* later published a letter from one of the other competitors, demanding court action for the return of his expenses because, in his opinion, the outcome had been a foregone conclusion.

The lowest tender for the building costs, from William Shepherd of Bermondsey, was £10,520. The work was completed in 1877, at a total cost of £18,500 6s 3d, including the cost of the land; the whole being met from public subscription.

As described by *The Building News* of 15th November 1878, the Hall was faced with red Bracknell bricks, with dressings of Portland stone and the roofs covered with 'the Broomhall Company's brown tiles'. The tower, or campanile, surmounted a side staircase and had a side-entrance door, and contained the cisterns (the upper part was later demolished or destroyed). The basement contained kitchens and a lift (presumably a dumb waiter rather than for people) supplied by Archibald Smith and Co. of Leicester Square, along with muniment and store rooms, and 'a residence for the hall-keeper'. On the ground floor, to the left of the entrance hall, was the hall for the meetings of the vestrymen (confusingly, this as well as the building was called the vestry hall), and to the right the rather large offices of the parish surveyor. Around the main staircase were the business offices of the parish – the vestry clerk's offices, the burial board, medical officer of health, superintendent registrar – plus a 'retiring-room' for the vestrymen and a strong-room.

The fittings of the vestry hall (the room) in walnut and maroon leather, and those of the surveyor's and other offices, were made by a Mr Turpin of Bayswater. What is now our main hall and theatre on the first floor, and was then called the public hall, had a floor 'supplied with Dennett's arching, which has been treated ornamentally as a ceiling for the vestry hall under'. The principal halls, corridors and staircases were heated by a hot water system fitted by S Eale and Sons of Oxford Street. The public hall and principal staircase were lit by means of 'sun burners' – presumably the latest in gas lighting.

The new Hall was designed in the then fashionable Italianate style, and was widely admired in the locality and elsewhere. *The Builder* hailed 'the free common sense style of Classic suitable for the official departments of a parish vestry'. The *Hampstead and Highgate Express* considered that it presented 'a handsome and solid appearance', and was 'a decided ornament to that part of Haverstock Hill'.

Inevitably, there were also detractors. Its siting, south of the old town, was not popular with the traders, nor with some residents. Dr Lord, Hampstead's first Medical Officer of Health, while congratulating the Vestry on their grand new Town Hall, commented that in his opinion baths and wash-houses should come first; and a local resident called it the 'Hall of Extravagance' (notwithstanding the Vestrymen's efforts at economy).

And no self-respecting account of the Town Hall is complete without the more recent comment of Nikolaus Pevsner, in the 1952 London edition of *Buildings of England*: '...1875, by Kendall and Mew. Red brick and stone, Italianate. Crushingly mean; a disgrace to so prosperous and artistic a borough.' (It must be said that he was generally hard on London town halls.)

Gordon Maclean, a present-day Belsize resident and architect, is less harsh. In a recent publication he has called it a 'likeably solid, four-square presence, commanding the corner of Haverstock Hill and Belsize Avenue. Typically Victorian Italianate, but that was how things were in 1877 (what is it that these people have against Victorian Italianate?). The Vestrymen were apparently being careful

with the ratepayers' money, and they got a serviceable, cost-effective, functional building: good, plain, down-to-earth virtues.'

Maclean also finds some interesting and high-quality details. The exterior may be unsensational, he says, but inside 'there is much to enjoy'. 'The main staircase has a real civic flourish about it, with nice ironwork, and a good colourful tiled floor. The public hall and vestry hall are beautifully proportioned and well detailed spaces, with good classical features, doorways and mirrors, well suited to public meetings, concerts, receptions, wedding parties and so on.'

The building was completed in 1877, but there was no official public opening ceremony. The public hall was first used on the 17th of June 1878, for the Cambridge Local Examination for women, and the Vestry officials began moving into their new offices on the 24th, although even then the Hall was not yet finished. The first full Vestry meeting took place on the 4th of July.

The new building was by all accounts a success. According to the Hampstead antiquarian FE Baines, the 'Public Hall was in great request for balls and public meetings and a gross income of more than £500 a year is derivable from fees paid for its use'.

The Hall was extended in 1888, at a cost of £5,413 19s 7d, with the addition of a new committee room, a retiring room for musicians (for it became a popular concert venue) and other facilities.

On the formation of the LCC, also in 1888, the parish ceased to be in Middlesex and became part of London. (To mark the occasion, a new coat of arms was drawn up, an ingenious amalgam of the arms of the various lords of the manor: the Dean and Chapter of Westminster, and the Campden and Gainsborough families.) In 1900, the vestries themselves ceased to exist, and were replaced by borough councils, with new powers and duties.

Another major extension of offices was built onto the Hall in 1910, reflecting the increasing importance of local government. From now on the building ceased to be a Vestry Hall, and was officially known as the Town Hall. The first Mayor of Hampstead was Sir Henry Harben, chairman of the Provident Assurance Company.

Serving Hampstead

The last decades of the 19th century, local civic and community activity flourished, and the Vestry Hall became a popular and valuable venue for society meetings and musical performances. In the winter months between 1883 and 1888, it accommodated the weekly meetings of the Hampstead Parliamentary Debating Society. It was also used for regular meetings by the Heath Protection Society (now the Heath and Hampstead Society), the Hampstead Historical and Antiquarian Society, and the Hampstead Freemasons.

From 1885 until about 1903, Popular Concerts were given at the Hall six times a year. Leading participants included Richard Mühlfeld (for whom Brahms wrote the four of his late chamber works that had clarinet parts), the Bohemian String Quartet, the violinist and composer Joseph Joachim and the composer Arnold Bax.

More recent events at the Hall have been an annual Asian Arts Festival, art exhibitions including works by Hockney, Kitaj and Weight, tea dances (many older members of the community remember these with affection), performances by the Hampstead Choral Society, and what was described as 'the largest sale of natural history specimens the world has ever seen', ranging from fleas to stuffed elephants and camels.

Many famous names are registered in the Town Hall records. Among those married there at the Registry Office were Marie Lloyd (for the third time) and T S Eliot (his first, in 1915).

In 1916 Lytton Strachey was called before a tribunal chaired by the Mayor in the Council Chamber, to explain why he was a conscientious objector. Asked by the tribunal what he would do if he saw a German soldier raping his sister, he famously replied: 'I should try and come between them'. Following subsequent medical examination he was discharged.

On the evening of the 22nd of October 1938, police were called to break up fighting in the Town Hall during a fascist meeting addressed by William Joyce, who, as Lord Haw Haw, broadcast for the Nazis during the Second World War and was hanged for treason in 1945.

During the War, an Administration and Information Centre was set up at the Town Hall, which also became the ARP Control Room for the Borough, with an observation post on the roof. A Civil Defence Control room and Message Rooms for the area were established in a building erected in the grounds. These were staffed mainly by volunteers from the Council, and operated 24 hours a day from the beginning of the war, dealing with 600 'incidents' and handling a vast number of telephone calls and post-raid inquiries. Massive concrete air-raid shelters were built. There were several near misses from bombs, and three actually struck the building: one hit the campanile, another damaged the structure of the public hall and the third lodged unexploded in the roof over the vestry hall. (It seems likely that this was when the top of the campanile came down.)

Decline and rescue

In 1964, Hampstead lost its borough status and became part of the new super-borough of Camden. The LCC became the GLC, and the main seat of local government moved to the former St Pancras Town Hall.

Then, in the 1980s, Camden decided to realise some of its assets and to centralise all council services to the south

A photograph of 1890, looking down Haverstock Hill.

CAMDEN LOCAL HISTORY STUDIES
AND ARCHIVE CENTRE

of the borough. The Hall was declared surplus to requirements and run down. It continued in council use for borough-wide services such as registration of births and deaths, highway maintenance and finance, but, by the end, the main hall was in such a state of neglect that it was no longer available for public hire. On the 3rd of November 1994 the building was closed, after more than a century of constant use by the local authority and enjoyment by countless local residents.

There had been no local consultation; it was only from the *Ham & High* that the public learned Camden had been advised to sell the Hall.

As a large, old and 'difficult' building, it was likely to be, at best, bought by a single company for use as a prestigious head office. At worst – well, the Council had already contemplated its demolition at least once. To counter this threat, the Belsize Conservation Area Advisory Committee, Belsize Residents' Association, Heath and Hampstead Society and South End Green Association campaigned to protect the Hall. As a result, in the summer of 1994, the Department of National Heritage listed it Grade II as 'a fine early example of a London Vestry Hall'. (Its interior, it was noted, still contained many original details, including cornices, fireplaces, clocks, patterned floor tiles and the main staircase with its elaborate cast iron balusters.) The Belsize Conservation Area was also extended to include the Town Hall.

Camden's first formal consultation with the public was

The restored front façade.
PHOTOGRAPH BY IH STEWART

in October 1994, when a planning brief for the site was prepared and local groups invited to comment. By this time, the Council was already far advanced with plans for disposal, but its proposals were strongly opposed. Five local residents' groups (the Heath and Old Hampstead Society, the South End Green Association, the Belsize Residents' Association, the Hampstead Conservation Area Advisory Committee and the Belsize Conservation Area Advisory Committee) combined to organise a public

meeting on the 9th of January 1995. With the help and support of local councillors, they got the Town Hall re-opened especially for the occasion.

Over 200 people attended, and it was made abundantly clear to Camden Council that the people wanted the Town Hall to remain in public ownership, and to be used for the community and for a local presence for Council services. The Council's representative conceded that it had 'under-estimated' the strength of public feeling, and agreed to meet local representatives to discuss a way forward. A working party of the local conservation and amenity groups was set up to examine possible uses for the Hall.

They were put in touch with the InterChange Trust, a local educational charity that had been established in Camden for thirty years and had a successful record of providing arts and community facilities. The Trust needed new premises, and was felt to be an ideal body to be the main occupant and manager of the Hall.

In 1996, a bid for funding from the Lottery board was drawn up, with the support of Camden Council, and in August the Arts Council and Heritage Lottery Boards agreed to make a grant of £6.35 million. In a new spirit of partnership and cooperation, Camden donated a ninety-nine-year lease on the building. The working party became the Friends of Hampstead Town Hall, and Inter-Change was charged with raising £2.1 million of matching funding, as required under the terms of the Lottery Boards grant. That task was successfully completed in 2000.

Resurrection

The work on the Town Hall encompasses the restoration and modernisation of the main Victorian building and the Edwardian (1910) extension alongside Belsize Avenue, and a completely new extension to the south-west. All of this was designed by the architects Burrell Foley Fischer, and executed by Messrs Baxalls, contractors.

The entire building was stripped of its modern features, including false panelling, partitions and polystyrene ceilings. The enormously thick, reinforced concrete World War II bunkers at the rear of the building were demolished.

Then brick, stone, wood and metal were restored and plasterwork reinstated. Modern amenities were installed, of course, including three lifts and provision for visitors in wheelchairs: the whole complex now has extensive facilities for the disabled, children and the elderly.

Most splendidly, perhaps, the missing tower or campanile was rebuilt following the original drawings, its foundations having been identified during detailed inspection of the building.

When the Hall was built, the prevailing style of decoration in public buildings tended to dark colours – chocolate brown, sage green, bottle green. Examination of the unrestored building revealed only some of the building's Victorian history, however, so these sombre shades are confined to two areas. The main entrance vestibule, with its blue, yellow and brown encaustic floor tiles, has been restored in autumnal colours, and what is now the main hall has been repainted in bottle green.

The remaining Vestry Hall rooms have been restored in a less solemn style, with walls painted ivory and complemented by white plaster ceilings and dentilled cornices.

Early photographs of the vestry hall, small hall and main staircase showed the original metal chandeliers, and have allowed them to be replaced with replicas.

The new wing is an entirely twentieth-century building. It is raised on stilts and a tall, simple plinth, which will be heavily planted to give the effect of 'earthing' the ground floor, with contrasting, lightweight and airy dance studios 'floating' above it. The studios are clad in a timber that is designed to weather to a silver grey, which will relate to the colour of the stone dressings of the main building. Between this wing and the Edwardian extension there is a high, glazed atrium, beautiful, spacious and light, evoking a Victorian conservatory.

There are also plans to exhibit sculpture and other works of art in the building – Sir Anthony Caro's *Black Russian*, which he has most generously donated to the Town Hall, is already in place.

The former public hall is now a 150-seat theatre and concert hall, and will once again become available for hire for concerts, drama and other events. The smaller, former

The main staircase as restored.   PHOTOGRAPH BY RICHARD DAVIS

vestry hall on the ground floor is equipped for debates, conferences and functions.

In the new wing is the arts and media centre, which contains two large dance studios and four sound-proofed music rehearsal rooms, three multi-media studios for sound recording and video editing, plus graphics and computer training facilities and an Internet suite. There is a particular focus in the arts centre on facilities for disabled young people.

The Edwardian building of 1910 accommodates the headquarters of the University of the Third Age, InterChange's headquarter offices, and offices for fifteen London charities, mostly offering community services to such pensioners, disabled people, single parents, refugees, arts groups and the like. It also contains a new 'town room' for community meetings, business meetings and training courses.

The main occupant and manager of the Town Hall is InterChange Studios, under the continuing energetic direction of Dr Alan Tomkins.

The future

Not everyone will be comfortable with the juxtaposition of the old and new buildings. Certainly the new wing does not mirror the Victorian Hall in style as the Edwardian extension does. Nevertheless there is, in their separation and in the simplicity of the new part, a sort of respect. The work serves, too, to remind us that conservation and new building can co-exist. A neighbourhood that rejects even the best of changes may become a desiccated theme park, just as one that rejects the past becomes rootless, shallow and dull.

The most important thing is that Hampstead Town Hall now has a future. It has been restored in a dignified and skilful way (as Ian Stewart says above, there are craftsmen still), and it has been secured for the renewed use and enjoyment of the community, at least for the next ninety-eight years. Is that too far ahead to be looking? Probably not. Ninety-eight years after the Vestrymen first moved in, it was on the brink of demolition.

But for now, there is good reason for optimism. InterChange Trust, inheritors of the Victorian spirit of practical charitable work, have been entrusted with the running, conservation and development of the new centre. They are committed to raising the £580,000 a year that that will cost, and to ensuring that Belsize – and Hampstead, Camden and London – have a fine, living building, and a new centre to be proud of.

PEOPLE POWER IN BELSIZE – DOES IT EXIST?

Conservation campaigns have played an important part in establishing the identity of Belsize. The attempt to save Belsize Wood is rightly characterised in Jake Brown's article above as a deeply held expression of collective opinion.

Early in the 1970s, the late Jim Stirling, even in those days an eminent and imposing figure, came from house to house saying, "Have you heard about the Motorway Box? We've got to do something." We did. The whole neighbourhood roused itself, along with other groups along the line of this madcap scheme, which would have slashed into vast residential districts right round London in order to build an inner ring motorway. We cannot claim to have defeated the scheme single-handed. It was a London-wide campaign that finally won the day. But it is sobering to think that if it had gone ahead it would have cut Belsize in two and altered it completely. The motorway would have crossed Finchley Road near the top of Maresfield Gardens and curved down to cross Belsize Park, passing down Belsize Square and towards Chalk Farm, sweeping away great swathes of houses. No St Peter's Church, no Synagogue. Even the alternative, and vastly expensive, option of tunnelling or cut-and-cover would have caused great disruption.

The local spirit aroused then came into play again a few years later, in rejecting the Council's attempt to channel all through traffic onto a selected network of roads by means

The needless destruction of an original nineteenth-century greenhouse (once owned by a famous gardener) at 116 Haverstock Hill. PHOTOGRAPH BY GENE ADAMS

of road closures. From this joint venture resulted the Three Roads Association, which later became the Belsize Residents' Association.

Since then, certain large issues have continued to stir people, and to call forth the sense of rightness which is the

Max Nasatyr and Mary Shenai

hallmark of people power. The campaign to save the Town Hall has been a tremendous unifying link in the neighbourhood. That story is told elsewhere in this volume. Less well remembered is the campaign, which started in 1974, to rescue 104-124 Haverstock Hill, part of a fine group of houses built by William Lund in the 1860s, reaching from the 'Load of Hay' up to and beyond Parkhill road. Numbers 114 and 116 are of particular importance, as they are visible from the entire length of England's Lane. In addition, number 116 was graced with a particularly fine Victorian conservatory. Number 112 was by then an empty site, where Daneshurst, a Gothic revival mansion, had been demolished some ten years before. All these houses, with number 126, the back-land beyond it and the smaller group of four houses to the south of Parkhill Road, had been acquired by Camden Borough Council by compulsory purchase. Camden now claimed that all the houses were in poor condition, that numbers 114 to 124 should be demolished immediately, and that the whole site north of Parkhill Road would be redeveloped.

Their architects produced a fearsome plan for a single block of flats on the site of numbers 112 to 124. Numerous people then joined a campaign and petitioned the Council to keep the houses.

For some time before this, the Belsize Residents' Association had received many requests for help from homeless young people, and in 1977 they managed to set up an innovative cooperative, Belpark, which aimed '(1) to provide affordable housing for local people in need, (2) to give people control of their housing in a supportive environment and (3) to make use of existing buildings which are either left empty or allowed to decay.' Funding for such a cooperative could be sought from the Housing Corporation. It would be run independently of the local authority, but would need its approval. Seven members of the Residents' Association, none of whom had any financial interest in the scheme, were to be founder members.

The larger site, consisting of the houses to the north of Parkhill Road, was to be the first venture, but how were Camden to be induced to give up their scheme? An architect member of the recently formed Belsize Conservation Area Advisory Committee, the late Pamela Banchero, had already worked tirelessly in the attempt to save 114-116, and she drew up and costed a scheme to restore the houses and convert them into small units suitable for single people. This scheme received unofficial approval from the Department of the Environment, and was put to the Council, with the apparent support of Ken Livingstone, who was then the chairman of Camden's housing committee. In fact, when the committee vote was evenly divided on the furiously contested issue of demolishing numbers 114, 116 and other houses in Haverstock Hill, Ken Livingstone 'used his casting vote to pass the recommendation for demolition' (*Ham & High*, 27th October 1979. In the ensuing stalemate, the houses were not demolished, but left to deteriorate for another fifteen years.

However, a surprise was in store, for the Council evidently had been impressed by the possibilities of Pamela Banchero's scheme, which had shown that houses could be converted into small units and still keep within the prescribed costing limits. They offered Belpark the possibility of submitting a similar scheme for the houses south of Parkhill Road. This was a challenge not to be missed.

Fortunately 104-110 were in a somewhat better condition than 114-116, as they had not been made uninhabitable by the council preparing for demolition. Moreover, they had been well maintained by squatters, who would now need to become functioning members of the Cooperative. With some trepidation, a meeting was arranged with the squatters, and from then on the scheme

Camden sends in the bulldozers

Protesters try to save houses for homeless

THE BULLDOZERS are set to move in on three houses in Hampstead later this month after Camden Council announced it has given up hope of using the buildings to house the homeless.

Last Thursday's meeting of the housing executive sub-committee decided to go ahead with the demolition of the houses in Belsize Avenue because of the cost of keeping them secure from squatters and the risk of losing £1.7 million in slum clearance cash from the Government.

The council vigorously defended its decision in the face of protests from local residents and homeless campaigners, who claim that the buildings should stay up until concrete plans for new housing on the site are in place.

The three houses were bought by the council under a compulsory purchase order in 1988 and it argues that demolition is required because the properties are structurally unsound and cannot not be "rehabilitated economically".

Last week Ernest James, Labour councillor and former chairman of the development control sub-committee, hit out at his party's plans by claiming that the houses were structurally sound and more time should be given to find a new landlord.

It is understood that the planning department failed in its attempts to persuade housing officers that the houses should be reprieved on planning grounds.

Charlie Hedges, chairman of the housing committee, said: "Camden tried, unsuccessfully, to market the properties, and looked into a range of options in great detail, none of which proved viable. Every possible avenue to obtaining a short-life scheme on this site was explored and no new route was discovered.

"In fact each option that we looked into confirmed the earlier position that we had no option but to demolish these premises, including advice from the Empty Homes Agency."

He said that over the last two years Camden had sought to enter into a 10-year lease with two housing associations by using its powers under Section 301 of the 1985 Housing Act to postpone demolition, but the Department of the Environment received legal advice that Camden's proposal would not be lawful.

It is now almost three years since squatters were evicted from the houses, and the housing department says that the cost of securing the houses is escalating, with the security fees from 1990 to 1993 alone amounting to nearly £300,000.

"There can be no further reason to delay demolition and disposal, as every effort to keep the properties in use has failed. We have bent over backwards in an attempt to avoid demolishing these properties," Mr Hedges said.

After the scaffolding went up over the weekend, Leonie Findlay, of the Belsize Park Conservation Area Advisory Committee, staged a demonstration with residents and former squatters on Monday. She said: "The council should not do anything like this until a real replacement has been agreed. It can't just pull these houses down at will."

● Protesters (from left) Gene Adams, Leonie Findlay, Margrit Mellows, Andrew Moore, Frank Mellows and Nick Moore.

Direct action in Belsize: local conservationists joined forces with campaigners against homelessness to fight Camden Council.

COURTESY OF HAMPSTEAD & HIGHGATE EXPRESS

started to become a reality. The Cooperative's managing committee now consisted of occupants of the houses and four members of the Residents Association, who later withdrew. A great deal of the future success of the scheme was due to the lucky chance that two of the squatters were young practising architects, and that some of the others were people with professional expertise. Thus its committee started with a great advantage. However, years of patient negotiation lay before them. This was hard work, real grass-roots democracy in action. Plans were drawn up

and, supported by reams of financial statements, they eventually secured Housing Corporation backing. In the face of all this, Camden Council agreed to negotiate thirty-year leases on 104-110 to enable the restoration of those houses to take place. Eventually the houses were occupied by the erstwhile squatters, along with additional and replacement members from Camden's housing waiting list.

Some time after the formation of the Belpark co-operative the Council, which could no longer afford to undertake large-scale developments, decided that the land

Left: Belsize Avenue was the worse for the loss of 53-59, and further degraded by their replacements.

Right: Nos. 53-59 Belsize Avenue were part of a remarkably complete and architecturally interesting row of houses.

PHOTOGRAPHS BY GENE ADAMS

behind 126 (the so called 'salt store') should be sold for private development, and that the houses to the north of Parkhill Road should be reinvestigated to see whether any restoration was possible along the same lines as the Belpark scheme. As a result Belpark Two was formed under the auspices of the original cooperative, which became Belpark One. The result is the major combined restoration and newly built development that stands there today. Nearly twenty years had elapsed from the time the houses were first threatened. Now 114 and 116, almost in their original form, still gaze down the length of England's Lane, secure for the foreseeable future.

It must be admitted that Camden's change of heart on the restoration of these buildings was influenced considerably by the drying up of funds for local authority housing projects and the need to tap other sources to secure affordable housing. Nevertheless, people power played a part by being in the right place at the right time.

So, does people power really exist in Belsize? Well, yes and no. Certainly it seems to have done so in the case of the Motorway Box, the Town Hall and Belpark. But it does not always succeed. Besides, Camden is getting cleverer at forestalling it: at 53-59 Belsize Avenue, which could have been restored in the same way as the Belpark houses, the squatters were forcibly evicted and the houses demolished. The rebuilding that took place there, a group of four houses attempting to fit in with limited success (betrayed by their deformed porches, short and fat), is occupied by leaseholders of flats instead of cooperative members of affordable housing. At the Swiss Cottage civic and open

*The reward of
conservation
campaigning: 114
and 116 Haverstock
Hill, almost in their
original form, remain
a landmark at the end
of England's Lane.*

PHOTOGRAPH BY
MARY SHENAI

space site, no proper public consultation on the placing of the new theatre took place until after outline planning permission (that immutable decision) had been granted, allowing the theatre to move to the best part of the open space. Moreover the unexpected presence of 200 dwellings and their cars on this civic site is not being welcomed by local residents, though it is needed to finance the scheme.

Planning decisions are never easy, even the small ones – the usual day-to-day tasks of the Conservation Area Advisory Committee and the Council's planning officers.

As Celia Scott rightly says in her article above, "One would not want 'fitting in' to be applied so rigorously as to eliminate all contrasts of character." Such decisions require constant watchfulness and debate. What is essential for the living suburb is that its occupants bother to look around them and evaluate what they see.

BELSIZE PARK PEOPLE

A personal selection of noteworthy residents and visitors

William and Helen Allingham lived in Eldon House (now demolished) at the corner of Eldon Grove and Lyndhurst Road. William, the prolific poet, best remembered for 'Up the airy mountain, down the rushy glen', died here in 1889. His wife's watercolours, notably of country cottages, are still very popular. There is a tablet to her in Rosslyn Hill Chapel, and a notable collection of her work at the Hampstead Museum in Burgh House.

Robert Bevan was a leading artist with the Camden Town Group, dominated by Walter Sickert. He and his artist wife, Stanislawa de Karlowska, came to 14 Adamson Road in 1901 (blue plaque added, 2000): he died there in 1925. From his studio window (still visible) Bevan painted his well-known view of Adamson Road. His other pictures of Belsize Park included one of the Hall Junior School, where he sent his son: this famous painting is now in the Museum of London.

Agatha Christie lived in Lawn Road Flats in 1945.

John Drinkwater, poet and playwright, was an insurance clerk until his sudden success in the theatre with *Abraham Lincoln* in 1918. Two other chronicle plays followed, *Mary Stuart* and *Oliver Cromwell*, both published in 1921, when he was living at 10 Belsize Square.

John Evelyn visited Belsize House in 1676, when it belonged to Lord Wotton.

Sigmund Freud's first home when he came as a refugee to Britain in 1938 was at 39 Elsworthy Road. Later that year he moved to 20 Maresfield Gardens, where he died in 1939. His statue sits in Belsize Lane outside the Tavistock Clinic.

George Grossmith, co-author of *The Diary of a Nobody*, lived from 1857 at Manor Lodge, on the site of Haverstock School. He went to another local school called Massingham House, where his headmistress reported: 'I am afraid he will one day be a clown'. She was proved right twenty years later, when Grossmith created many of the comic leads in Gilbert and Sullivan operas: his patter songs were said to be the fastest in the West End.

Sir Rowland Hill is commemorated by a street name and a plaque near the Royal Free Hospital. The originator of the Penny Post lived here, in Bartram House (now demolished), for thirty years until his death in 1879. He had successfully opposed the building of a smallpox hospital nearby but, soon after his death, his estate was bought up and developed for the North West Fever Hospital in Lawn Road.

Sir Henry Isaacs, who lived at 27 Belsize Park, was a prosperous fruit broker who became Lord Mayor of London in 1889/90. 'A Jew of the purest type,' said the *Hampstead Yearbook* at the time, 'he is only the third man of that creed to occupy the civic throne.'

Jerome K. Jerome, who started as a railway clerk at Euston, moved to 41 Belsize Park in 1924. It was a prestigious address that suited the famous author of *Three Men in a Boat* and the sensational drama *The Passing of the Third Floor Back*. He worshipped with his wife at St Peter's and walked his dog on the Heath, but otherwise led a stay-at-home life, which was just what the doctor had ordered for this frail old man. His main work was the completion of his autobiography *My Life and Times*. Belsize Park was still his home when he died (actually in Northampton Hospital) in 1927.

Oscar Kokoschka, the Austrian artist, came to Britain as a refugee in 1938, and lived briefly and penuriously at 2A King Henry's Road, in a flat that belonged to a ventriloquist. He later moved to Mandeville Court in Finchley Road.

Christopher Wade

Editor's note: This article appeared in the 1986 edition of this book.

Marie Lloyd, the music-hall favourite, also lived in King Henry's Road, in 1906. Her home, No. 98, was on the site of the present Quickswood. She married her third husband at Hampstead Town Hall. Her modest grave can be seen in Hampstead Cemetery at Fortune Green.

Ramsay MacDonald, who came to 9 Howitt Road in 1916, was leader of the Labour Party in opposition from 1922, and prime minister in 1924. This was the first Labour government in Britain. The following year, he left Howitt Road for a bigger and better house, 103 Frognal, a move much criticised by many socialist supporters, who thought the new house too grand. Both houses now bear plaques to MacDonald.

H W Nevinson was a crusading journalist and eminent war correspondent, known in his profession as the Grand Duke. As he came from an old Hampstead family, it is not surprising that he lived at several local addresses, including 4 Downside Crescent around 1940. His son, CRW Nevinson, one of the few cubist war artists, died at 1 Steele's Studios in 1946.

George Orwell took a job in a bookshop at the foot of Pond Street in 1934, and lodged in Warwick Mansions next door. He was glad to be in Hampstead, as his weak chest needed the Heath's fresh air, and he welcomed this part-time job, which allowed him to pursue his writing. *Keep the Aspidistra Flying* includes some savage satire on local people and places. A private plaque now commemorates Orwell's brief stay here.

Spencer Perceval, who has left his name on Perceval Avenue, lived at Belsize House from 1798 to 1807. His parliamentary career prospered during this time, and by 1809 he became prime minister. Nobody remembers much about his term of office except its dramatic end: on entering the lobby of the House of Commons one day in 1812, he was shot dead by a madman, a bankrupt broker called John Bellingham.

Queen Victoria often enjoyed country drives in this area.

The **Earl of Rosslyn** began life as Alexander Wedderburn, and is commemorated in two local street names. He was a successful Scottish lawyer, who rose to be Chief Justice of Common Pleas by 1780. In that year, his harsh sentencing of the Gordon Rioters earned him the name of 'the second Judge Jeffreys'. In 1793 he became Lord Chancellor and in 1801 he came to a large mansion near the top of Lyndhurst Road, later known as Rosslyn House, and stayed there until his death in 1805. (Other Georgian Chancellors, Lords Lyndhurst, Eldon and Thurlow, inspired further street names on the Rosslyn Park Estate.)

Alfred Stevens, the artist and sculptor, lived at 9 Eton Villas (there is a blue plaque) from 1859 until his death in 1875. The last ten years of his life were devoted to designing and executing the vast monument to the Duke of Wellington in St Paul's, but he died before it was finished. Wellington House in Eton Road is on the site of a large house of that name that Stevens designed for himself.

S S Teulon was a 'rogue architect' of French Huguenot stock, which may help to explain his unconventional design for St Stephen's on Hampstead Green. He had already built or restored over a hundred other churches, including one in Avenue Road, which was destroyed in the last war, before completing St Stephen's in 1869. Teulon lived for many years at a nearby house called Tensleys (demolished) and here he died in 1873, exhausted by work on this church, which he considered his masterpiece. He is buried in Highgate Cemetery.

Violet Van der Elst lived at 30 Belsize Park from 1912 – and made her fortune there. She turned her kitchen into a face-cream factory and produced Doge Cream, 'based on an old Venetian recipe', and the first brushless shaving cream. When her husband died here mysteriously in 1927, she married their lodger and moved to Kensington. Soon after her second husband's death in 1934, she began a crusade for the abolition of capital punishment, appearing dramatically dressed in black outside every prison where an execution was imminent.

Sir Henry Wood was at 4 Elsworthy Road from 1905 to 1937, and is commemorated by a blue plaque. He became musical director of the Promenade Concerts (then at Queen's Hall) in 1895, and they soon became established as an annual event. His house in Elsworthy Road was much visited by Richard Strauss, Frederick Delius and other composers.

Among other notable residents of Belsize Park have been: **Richard Burton**, actor (Lyndhurst Road), **Dame Clara Butt**, singer (Harley Road), **Florrie Forde**, music hall artist (Haverstock Hill), **Duncan Grant**, artist (Fellows Road), **Sir Alexander Korda**, film producer (Avenue Road), **Piet Mondrian**, artist (Parkhill Road), **Arthur Rackham**, illustrator (Chalcot Gardens), **Sir Richard Steele**, writer (near Steele's Road), **Lytton Strachey**, writer (Belsize Park Gardens) and **Twiggy**, model (Belsize Crescent).

CONTRIBUTORS

Roy Allen has done, and is still doing, research into the early history of Belsize, and has contributed a number of articles to *Camden History Review*.

The late **Gwen Barnard** was a painter and print-maker. She was chairman of Womens International Art Club, 1960–64, and lived in Mall Studios for many years.

Michael Brod is an architect living and practising in Belsize, and has a close association with the Belsize Synagogue.

Jake Brown is an architect, and was a long-time member of the RIBA Council; worked for many years in the GLC's Architecture Department and in private practice and with a Hospital Board. Former chairman of the Belsize Conservation Advisory Committee. Initiated and until recently chaired the Greater London Architecture Club.

Leonie Findlay (née Cohn) was Chairman of the Belsize CAAC from 1987 to 1995. Before that, she played a crucial role in the creation of the 1986 book and exhibition by Belsize CAAC, held in Hampstead Town Hall. Leonie worked for many years for BBC Radio. After retiring, she specialised in interviews with prominent members in the world of art and architecture. Her long friendship with the distinguished Read family dated from the late 1930s, when, as a young refugee from Nazi Germany, she worked for Herbert (later Sir Herbert) and Margaret Read.

Michael Hammerson is chairman of the Highgate Society's Environment Committee. His interests include local history, and he has made a special study of the American Civil War. During three years as deputy curator of Hampstead Museum, he followed the story of the Rev F W Tremlett, and is continuing this research.

Gerry Harrison is a local councillor (the Isokon building is in his ward), and a producer of films and television programmes.

Howard Isenberg is an ex-schoolteacher and a life-long resident of Hampstead. He has a long and active association with St Peter's, Belsize Square.

Leon Krier is an architect and urbanist. Born in Luxembourg in 1946, he has lived in England since 1968. He worked intermittently with James Stirling, 1968–1974. In private practice since 1974, he was a lecturer at the Architectural Association School, Royal College of Art and Princeton, US. Buildings at St Quentin-Ivelines, France and in Berlin. Publications: *The Reconstruction of the European City*; *The Consumption of Culture*; *Architects, Private Virtues and Public Vices*.

Max Nasatyr is an architect in private practice, and a resident in Belsize Park for 35 years. He is a founder member and former chairman of the Belsize Residents' Association, a founder member of Belpark and a member of the Belsize Conservation Area Advisory Committee.

The late **Jack Pritchard**, OBE and Honorary Fellow of the RIBA, was an early enthusiast for modern design and architecture. He was founder and head of the Isokon Furniture Company, for which Marcel Breuer designed the Long Chair, etc. Ministry of Supply 1941–44, Ministry of Fuel and Power, engaged in post-war planning, 1944. Director of the Furniture Development Council, 1949–56.

Andrew Saint is a distinguished architectural historian, was a member of the GLC Historic Buildings Division and is the author of a biography of Norman Shaw.

Celia Scott is an architect, and Principal of Maxwell Scott Architects. She has been a resident of Belsize Park since 1975.

Deirdre Sharp is Curator of Archive Collections at the University of East Anglia, Norwich.

Mary Shenai is a retired doctor, and a Belsize resident since 1958. She is a founder member of both the Belsize Residents' Association and the Belsize Conservation Area Advisory Committee. Her original research into the builders Tidey and Willett brings together new information about them and their families.

Adrian Shire used to be a publisher, but thought better of it, and is now an independent editor and writer. He is active in the local amenity movement.

Robin Spence, partner in Spence and Webster, architects. Among their designs and buildings are a new parliament building (project) and Rosshall Hospital, Glasgow.

Ian Stewart is an historic buildings architect in private practice and a Belsize resident who takes a keen interest in the local environment. His firm recently oversaw the restoration of Belsize Fire Station.

The late **Sir John Summerson** lived in Belsize for many years and was an architectural historian and a curator of the Sir John Soane Museum. Among his many publications are *Architecture in Britain 1530–1830, Architecture Here and Now, Victorian Architecture, The Classical Language of Architecture, Georgian London* and *The Life and Work of John Nash*.

Michael L Taylor BA (Hons) Arch. trained as an architect but spent most of his career with the RIBA as a director of RIBA Services, working on information systems. He is now chairman of the St Stephen's Restoration and Preservation Trust.

Christopher Wade is active in the Camden History Society. Published his survey *The Streets of Hampstead*, among others, in conjunction with High Hill Press. Founder of the Hampstead Museum at Burgh House.

APPENDIX I

The work of the Belsize Conservation Area Advisory Committee

'Conservation area advisory committees (CAACs) have their origins in the Town and Country Planning Act 1968 (Circular 61/68), the idea being that a high level of participation and help would assist in the Council's designation, protection and enhancement of conservation areas.

'Whilst CAACs have no statutory function, Government advice as set out in PPG15 (Planning and the Historic Environment) advises local planning authorities 'to consider setting up conservation area advisory committees to assist in formulating policies for the conservation area... and also as a continuing source of advice on planning and other applications that would affect the area.' Membership should comprise residents, councillors, business people and representatives from professional bodies and amenity societies. Whilst the Council is not required to set up CAACs, they have formed a distinctive part of planning in Camden since 1968.'

Camden's fourteen CAACs 'perform as fully independent entities which have developed a variety of different patterns of membership and working arrangements operating at 'arms length' from the Council'.

'The major strength of many CAACs is that they have built up considerable expertise and local knowledge of their areas over many years. The CAACs provide an extremely valuable service to the Council, which includes providing advice on planning applications and traffic management schemes through to consultation and participation in the designation of conservation areas and the preparation of conservation area statements... The CAACs provide local contacts within the community, have a long-term commitment to the area and are a source of everyday monitoring. Essentially the CAACs provide detailed local knowledge and interest that complement the specialist advice provided by officers.'

From a report to the Environment (Development Control) Subcommittee, London Borough of Camden, 8th July 1999.

Belsize CAAC consists of eleven long–standing residents, some of whom have worked on this committee since its inception in the early 1970s.

The work is voluntary and entirely self–funded. The members meet at least once every three weeks throughout the year – or more frequently – to inspect and advise upon current planning applications within the four Belsize conservation areas – Belsize Park, Parkhill and Upper Park, and Elsworthy. This regular work involves studying the relevant plans, visiting the sites and following the progress of applications through correspondence. We have also commented on the Draft Unitary Development Plan formulated by the Council to guide and assist all planning applications, and on specific conservation area statements. Sometimes we mount campaigns on specific buildings such as the saving and restoration of Nos. 114-116 Haverstock Hill in the 1970s, and the saving and transformation, with the aid of all other major amenity societies, of Hampstead Town Hall.

It was in addition to its usual work that Belsize CAAC decided to raise a special fund to create an exhibition of photographs and publish this book.

Our aim is to raise local consciousness. Our message is directed specially towards the next generation. Which of you is ready to take up the torch, and give some of your skills and energy towards enhancing and conserving for posterity your unique local environment?

APPENDIX II

Further Reading

The Classical Language of Architecture, Sir John Summerson, The MIT Press/Thames & Hudson Ltd

Greek Art, John Boardman, World of Art Library, Thames and Hudson

Victorian Architecture, Roger Dixon and Stefan Muthesius, World of Art Library, Thames and Hudson

Edwardian Architecture, Alastair Service, World of Art Library, Thames and Hudson

Hampstead: Building a Borough, 1650–1964, FML Thompson, Routledge and Kegan Paul

Streets of Hampstead and Streets of Belsize, both Camden History Society, edited by Christopher Wade, High Hill Press

Putting Back the Style, ed. Alexandra Artley, Evans

The English House Through Seven Centuries, Olive Cook, Nelson

The English House, H H Tipping, Country Life

The Architecture of the Renaissance, Benevolo, Routledge and Kegan Paul

Royal Greenwich, Nigel Hamilton, The Greenwich Bookshop

Renaissance Architecture of Venice, Ralph Lieberman, Frederick Muller

Islamic Architecture, Harry N Abrams, Electra Editions (Milan)

Buildings of England: London excluding the cities of London and Westminster, Nicholas Pevsner, Penguin Books

Richard Norman Shaw, Andrew Saint, Yale University Press

Hampstead One Thousand, AD 986–1986, John Richardson, Historical Publications with the London Borough of Camden

Bedford Park, the first Garden Suburb: a pictorial survey, T Afleck Greeves, Bingley

Evolution of the House, Stephen Gardiner, Paladin

The Care of Old Buildings Today, Donald Insall, Architectural Press

Victorian Architecture, Robert Furneaux Jordan, Penguin

The English Terraced House, Stephen Muthesius, Yale University Press

Dream House: The Edwardian Ideal, Roderick Gradidge, Constable

Architectural Journal's Housing Rehabilitation Handbook, Architectural Press

How to restore and improve your Victorian House, Alan Johnson, David & Charles

The Decoration of the Suburban Villa, 1880–1940, Mark Turner, William Riddick and Graham Dalling, Middlesex Polytechnic

Arts and Crafts Architecture: the Search for Earthly Paradise, Peter Davey, Architectural Press

Sweetness and Light: the Queen Anne Movement, 1860–1900, Mark Girouard, Yale University Press

View from a Long Chair: The Memoirs of Jack Pritchard, Routledge and Kegan Paul

Victorian Pubs, Mark Girouard, Yale University Press

The 1871 and 1881 census on microfilm at the Camden local history archive; also street directories from 1873 onwards.

An Isokon bibliography

Sherban Cantacuzino, *Wells Coates, a monograph*, 1978

Laura Cohn (ed.), *Wells Coates, Architect and Designer*, 1895–1958 Oxford Polytechnic Press, 1979

Laura Cohn, *The Door to a Secret Room. A Portrait of Wells Coates*, Scolar Press, 1999

Alistair Grieve, 'Isokon'; an article in the catalogue to an exhibition, *Hampstead in the Thirties*, ed. Michael Collins, 1974

Periodicals

The Architect and Building News, August 1934

The Architects Journal, June 1933, September 1934, May 1935

The Architectural Review, August 1934, September 1934, December 1935

Art and Architecture News, February 2000

The Builder, July 1934

Building, August 1934

Building Design, December 1997 and various

Building Times, August 1934

Camden History Review, October 1966

Concrete, 1934

doc-co-mo-mo newsletter, 1993 and various

Newspapers

The Hampstead and Highgate Express, various

The Camden New Journal, various

The Camden Chronicle, various

Evening Standard, 'Building Blocks' (Jennifer Potter March 2000), 'A Modernist Haven' (Libby Annat, May 2000)

The Sunday Times, 'Upstart' (Tim Kirby, date?)

The Observer, 'An End to Utopia' (Kenneth Powell, date?)

Writers' Block, article by Naomi Stungp (January 1999)

The Guardian Space Magazine, 'Modern Decline' (Pamela Buxton, January 1999)

Obituaries of Jack Pritchard, various newspapers (April 1992)